R. D. LAING

The Politics of Experience
and
The Bird of Paradise

PENGUIN BOOKS

Penguin Books Ltd, Harmondsworth, Middlesex, England
Penguin Books, 625 Madison Avenue, New York, New York 10022, U.S.A.
Penguin Books Australia Ltd, Ringwood, Victoria, Australia
Penguin Books Canada Ltd, 41 Steelcase Road West, Markham, Ontario, Canada
Penguin Books (N.Z.) Ltd, 182–190 Wairau Road, Auckland 10, New Zealand

—

First published 1967
Reprinted 1968, 1969, 1970 (twice), 1971, 1972, 1973, 1974, 1975, 1977

—

—

Made and printed in Great Britain by
Hazell Watson & Viney Ltd,
Aylesbury, Bucks
Set in Monotype Times

For my children

Contents

Acknowledgements

This book has been written over the past three years. Earlier versions of parts of it were published, or given as lectures, as follows:

Chapter 2
This is a revised version of a speech to the Sixth International Congress of Psychotherapy, London, 1964, entitled 'Practice and Theory: The Present Situation'. Reprinted in *Psychother. Psychosom.*, 13: 58–67 (1965).

Chapter 3
Part of Chapter 3 is a revised version of a lecture given at the Institute of Contemporary Arts, London, 1964. Reprinted as 'Violence and Love' in the *Journ. of Existentialism*, Volume 5, Number 20 (1965) and as 'Massacre of the Innocents' in *Peace News*, Number 1491 (1965).

Chapter 4
Part of Chapter 4 is a revised version of 'Series and Nexus in the Family' which appeared in *New Left Review*, 15 (1962).

Chapter 5
Earlier versions of this chapter have appeared as: 'What is Schizophrenia?', speech to the First International Congress of Social Psychiatry, London, 1964; 'What is Schizophrenia?' *New Left Review*, 28:63 (1964); 'Is Schizophrenia a Disease?' *Int. Journ. Soc. Psy.*, Volume X, Number 3, 1964.

Chapter 6
This is based on a paper delivered to the First International Congress of Social Psychiatry, London, 1964, entitled 'Transcendental Experience in Relation to Religion and Psychosis'. Reprinted in *Psychedelic Review*, No. 6, 1965.

ACKNOWLEDGEMENTS

Chapter 7

This is a revised version of an article entitled 'A Ten-Day Voyage' which appeared in *Views*, Number 8 (1965).

Introduction

FEW books today are forgivable. Black on the canvas, silence on the screen, an empty white sheet of paper, are perhaps feasible. There is little conjunction of truth and social 'reality'. Around us are pseudo-events, to which we adjust with a false consciousness adapted to see these events as true and real, and even as beautiful. In the society of men the truth resides now less in what things are than in what they are not. Our social realities are so ugly if seen in the light of exiled truth, and beauty is almost no longer possible if it is not a lie.

What is to be done? We who are still half alive, living in the often fibrillating heartland of a senescent capitalism – can we do more than reflect the decay around and within us? Can we do more than sing our sad and bitter songs of disillusion and defeat?*

The requirement of the present, the failure of the past, is the same: to provide a thoroughly self-conscious and self-critical human account of man.

No one can begin to think, feel or act now except from the starting-point of his or her own alienation. We shall examine some of its forms in the following pages.

We are all murderers and prostitutes – no matter to what culture, society, class, nation one belongs, no matter how normal, moral or mature one takes oneself to be.

Humanity is estranged from its authentic possibilities. This basic vision prevents us from taking any unequivocal

* It may be that dialectical theory finds its present truth in its own hopelessness. See Herbert Marcuse, *One-Dimensional Man* (London: Routledge & Kegan Paul, 1964). This is not my view.

view of the sanity of common sense, or of the madness of the so-called madman.* However, what is required is more than a passionate outcry of outraged humanity.

Our alienation goes to the roots. The realization of this is the essential springboard for any serious reflection on any aspect of present inter-human life. Viewed from different perspectives, construed in different ways and expressed in different idioms, this realization unites men as diverse as Marx, Kierkegaard, Nietzsche, Freud, Heidegger, Tillich and Sartre.†

We are bemused and crazed creatures, strangers to our true selves, to one another, and to the spiritual and material world – mad, even, from an ideal standpoint we can glimpse but not adopt.

We are born into a world where alienation awaits us. We are potentially men, but are in an alienated state, and this state is not simply a natural system. Alienation as our present destiny is achieved only by outrageous violence perpetrated by human beings on human beings.

* For a scholarly analysis of alienation in sociological and clinical senses, see Joseph Gabel, *La Fausse Conscience* (Paris: Les Éditions de Minuit, 1962).

See also Michel Foucault, *Madness and Civilisation* (New York: Pantheon Books, 1965; London: Tavistock Publications, 1966).

† It is too late in the day now to go over the ground again covered by the thinkers of the last 150 years who have spelled out the nature of alienation, especially in relation to capitalism. For a succinct summary, see Ernst Fischer, *The Necessity of Art* (London: Penguin Books, 1963), especially Chapter 3, 'Art and Capitalism'.

The Politics of Experience

Chapter 1

Persons and Experience

... that great and true Amphibian whose nature is disposed to live, not only like other creatures in divers elements, but in divided and distinguished worlds.

SIR THOMAS BROWNE, *Religio Medici*

I. Experience as evidence

EVEN facts become fictions without adequate ways of seeing 'the facts'. We do not need theories so much as the experience that is the source of the theory. We are not satisfied with faith, in the sense of an implausible hypothesis irrationally held: we demand to experience the 'evidence'.

We can see other people's behaviour, but not their experience. This has led some people to insist that psychology has nothing to do with the other person's experience, but only with his behaviour.

The other person's behaviour is an experience of mine. My behaviour is an experience of the other. The task of social phenomenology is to relate my experience of the other's behaviour to the other's experience of my behaviour. Its study is the relation between experience and experience: its true field is *inter-experience*.

I see you, and you see me. I experience you, and you experience me. I see your behaviour. You see my behaviour. But I do not and never have and never will see your *experience* of me. Just as you cannot 'see' my experience of you. My experience of you is not 'inside' me. It is simply you, as I experience you. And I do not experience you as inside me. Similarly, I take it that you do not experience me as inside you.

15

'My experience of you' is just another form of words for 'you-as-I-experience-you', and 'your experience of me' equals 'me-as-you-experience-me'. Your experience of me is not inside you and my experience of you is not inside me, but *your experience of me is invisible to me and my experience of you is invisible to you.*

I cannot experience your experience. You cannot experience my experience. We are both invisible men. All men are invisible to one another. Experience used to be called The Soul. Experience as invisibility of man to man is at the same time more evident than anything. *Only* experience is evident. Experience is the *only* evidence. Psychology is the logos of experience. Psychology is the structure of the *evidence*, and hence psychology is the science of sciences.

If, however, experience is evidence, how can one ever study the experience *of the other*? For the experience *of the other* is not evident to me, as it is not and never can be an experience of mine.

I cannot avoid trying to understand your experience, because although I do not experience your experience, which is invisible to me (and non-tasteable, non-touchable, non-smellable, and inaudible), yet I experience you *as experiencing*.

I do not experience your experience. But I experience you as experiencing. I experience myself as experienced by you. And I experience you as experiencing yourself as experienced by me. And so on.

The study of the experience of others, is based on inferences I make, from my experience of you experiencing me, about how you are experiencing me experiencing you experiencing me. . . .

Social phenomenology is the science of my own and of others' *experience*. It is concerned with the relation between my experience of you and your experience of me. That is, with *inter-experience*. It is concerned with your behaviour and my behaviour *as I experience it*, and your and my behaviour *as you experience it*.

Since your and their experience is invisible to me as mine is to you and them, I seek to make evident to the others, through their experience of my behaviour, what I infer of your experience, through my experience of your behaviour.

This is the crux of social phenomenology.

Natural science is concerned only with the observer's experience of things. Never with the way things *experience us*. That is not to say that things do not react to us, and to each other.

Natural science knows nothing of the relation between behaviour and experience. The nature of this relation is mysterious – in Marcel's sense. That is to say, it is not an objective problem. There is no traditional logic to express it. There is no developed method of understanding its nature. But this relation is the copula of our science – if science means *a form of knowledge adequate to its subject*. The relation between experience and behaviour is the stone that the builders will reject at their peril. Without it the whole structure of our theory and practice must collapse.

Experience is invisible to the other. But experience is not 'subjective' rather than 'objective', not 'inner' rather than 'outer', not process rather than praxis, not input rather than output, not psychic rather than somatic, not some doubtful data dredged up from introspection rather than extrospection. Least of all is experience 'intra-psychic process'. Such transactions, object-relations, interpersonal relations, transference, counter-transference, as we suppose to go on between people are not the interplay merely of two objects in space, each equipped with ongoing intra-psychic processes.

This distinction between outer and inner usually refers to the distinction between behaviour and experience; but sometimes it refers to some experiences that are supposed to be 'inner' in contrast to others that are 'outer'. More accurately this is a distinction between different modalities of experience, namely, perception (as outer) in contrast to imagination etc. (as inner). But perception, imagination, phantasy, reverie, dreams, memory, are simply different *modalities of experience*, none more 'inner' or 'outer' than any others.

Yet this way of talking does reflect a split in our experience. We seem to live in two worlds, and many people are aware only of the 'outer' rump. As long as we remember that the 'inner' world is not some space 'inside' the body or the mind, this way of talking can serve our purpose. (It was good enough for William Blake.) The 'inner', then, is our personal idiom of experiencing our bodies, other people, the animate and inanimate world: imagination, dreams, phantasy, and beyond that to ever further reaches of experience.

Bertrand Russell once remarked that the stars are in one's brain.

The stars as I perceive them are no more or less in my brain than the stars as I imagine them. I do not imagine them to be in my head, any more than I see them in my head.

The relation of experience to behaviour is not that of inner to outer. My experience is not inside my head. My experience of this room is out there in the room.

To say that my experience is intra-psychic is to presuppose that there is a psyche that my experience is in.

18

My psyche is my experience, my experience is my psyche.

Many people used to believe that angels moved the stars. It now appears that they do not. As a result of this and like revelations, many people do not now believe in angels.

Many people used to believe that the 'seat' of the soul was somewhere in the brain. Since brains began to be opened up frequently, no one has seen 'the soul'. As a result of this and like revelations, many people do not now believe in the soul.

Who could suppose that angels move the stars, or be so superstitious as to suppose that because one cannot see one's soul at the end of a microscope it does not exist?

II. Interpersonal experience and behaviour

Our task is both to experience and to conceive the concrete, that is to say, reality in its fullness and wholeness.

But this is quite impossible, immediately. Experientially and conceptually, we have fragments.

We can begin from concepts of the single person*, from the relations between two or more persons, from groups or from society at large; or from the material world, and

* Under person, the *Oxford English Dictionary* gives eight variants: a part played in a drama, or in life; an individual human being; the living body of a human being; the actual self of a human being; a human being or body corporate or corporation with rights or duties recognized in law; theologically applied, the three modes of the Divine Being in the Godhead; grammatically, each of the three classes of pronouns and corresponding distinctions in verbs denoting the person speaking, i.e. in the first, second, third person respectively, and so on; zoologically, each individual of a compound or colonial organism – a zooid.

As we are concerned here with human beings, our two most relevant variants are person as persona, mask, part being played; and person as actual self.

conceive of individuals as secondary. We can derive the main determinants of our individual and social behaviour from external exigencies. All these views are partial vistas and partial concepts. Theoretically one needs a spiral of expanding and contracting schemata that enable us to move freely and without discontinuity from varying degrees of abstraction to greater or lesser degrees of concreteness. Theory is the articulated vision of experience. This book begins and ends with the person.

Can human beings be persons today? Can a man be his actual self with another man or woman? Before we can ask such an optimistic question as 'What is a personal relationship?', we have to ask if a personal relationship is possible, or, *are persons possible* in our present situation? We are concerned with the possibility of man. This question can be asked only through its facets. Is love possible? Is freedom possible?

Whether or not all, or some, or no human beings are persons, I wish to define a person in a twofold way: in terms of experience, as a centre of orientation of the objective universe; and in terms of behaviour, as the origin of actions. Personal experience transforms a given field into a field of intention and action: only through action can our experience be transformed. It is tempting and facile to regard 'persons' as only separate objects in space, who can be studied as any other natural objects can be studied. But just as Kierkegaard remarked that one will never find consciousness by looking down a microscope at brain cells or anything else, so one will never find persons by studying persons as though they were only objects. A person is the me or you, he or she, whereby an object is experienced. Are these centres of experience, and origins of actions, living in entirely unrelated worlds of their own composition? Everyone must refer here to their own experience. My own experience as a centre of experience and origin of action tells me that this is not so. My experience and my action occur in a social field of reciprocal influence and interaction. I experience myself, identifiable as Ronald Laing by myself and others, as experienced by and acted upon by others, who refer to that person I call 'me' as 'you' or 'him', or grouped together as 'one of us' or 'one of them' or 'one of you'.

This feature of personal relations does not arise in the correlation of the behaviour of non-personal objects. Many social scientists deal with their embarrassment by denying its occasion. Nevertheless, the natural scientific world is complicated by the presence of certain identifiable entities, re-identifiable reliably over periods of years, whose behaviour is either the manifestation or a concealment of a view of the world equivalent in ontological status to that of the scientist.

People may be observed to sleep, eat, walk, talk, etc. in relatively predictable ways. We must not be content with observation of this kind alone. Observation of behaviour must be extended by inference to attributions about experience. Only when we can begin to do this can we really construct the experiential-behavioural system that is the human species.

It is quite possible to study the visible, audible, smellable effulgences of human bodies, and much study of human behaviour has been in those terms. One can lump together very large numbers of units of behaviour and regard them as a statistical population, in no way different from the multiplicity constituting a system of non-human objects. But one will not be studying persons. In a science of persons, I shall state as axiomatic that: behaviour is a function of experience; and both experience and behaviour are always in relation to someone or something other than self.

When two (or more) persons are in relation, the behaviour of each towards the other is mediated by the experience by each of the other, and the experience of each is mediated by the behaviour of each. There is no contiguity between the behaviour of one person and that of the other. Much human behaviour can be seen as unilateral or bilateral *attempts* to eliminate experience. A person may treat another *as though* he was not a person, and he may act himself *as though* he was not a person. There is no contiguity between one person's experience and another. My experience of you is always mediated through your *behaviour*. Behaviour that is the direct consequence of impact, as of one billiard-ball hitting another, or experience directly transmitted to experience, as in the possible cases of extra-sensory perception, is not personal.

III. *Normal alienation from experience*

The relevance of Freud to our time is largely his insight and, to a very considerable extent, his *demonstration* that the *ordinary* person is a shrivelled, desiccated fragment of what a person can be.

As adults, we have forgotten most of our childhood, not only its contents but its flavour; as men of the world, we hardly know of the existence of the inner world: we barely remember our dreams, and make little sense of them when we do; as for our bodies, we retain just sufficient proprioceptive sensations to coordinate our movements and to ensure the minimal requirements for biosocial survival – to register fatigue, signals for food, sex, defaecation, sleep; beyond that, little or nothing.

Our capacity to think, except in the service of what we are dangerously deluded in supposing is our self-interest, and in conformity with common sense, is pitifully limited: our capacity even to see, hear, touch, taste and smell is so shrouded in veils of mystification that an intensive discipline of un-learning is necessary for *anyone* before one can begin to experience the world afresh, with innocence, truth and love.

And immediate experience of, in contrast to belief or faith in, a spiritual realm of demons, spirits, Powers, Dominions, Principalities, Seraphim and Cherubim, the Light, is even more remote. As domains of experience become more alien to us, we need greater and greater open-mindedness even to conceive of their existence.

Many of us do not know, or even believe, that every night we enter zones of reality in which we forget our waking life as regularly as we forget our dreams when we awake. Not all psychologists know of phantasy as a modality of experience*, and the, as it were, contrapuntal interweaving of the different experiential modes. Many who are aware of phantasy believe that phantasy is the farthest that experience goes under 'normal' circumstances. Beyond that are simply 'pathological' zones of hallucinations, phantasmagoric mirages, delusions.

This state of affairs represents an almost unbelievable devastation of our experience. Then there is empty chatter about maturity, love, joy, peace.

This is itself a consequence of and further occasion for the divorce of our experience, such as is left of it, from our behaviour.

What we call 'normal' is a product of repression,

* See R. D. Laing, *The Self and Others* (London: Tavistock Publications, 1961; Chicago: Quadrangle Press, 1962) especially Part I.

23

denial, splitting, projection, introjection and other forms of destructive action on experience (see below). It is radically estranged from the structure of being.

The more one sees this, the more senseless it is to continue with generalized descriptions of supposedly specifically schizoid, schizophrenic, hysterical 'mechanisms'.

There are forms of alienation that are relatively strange to statistically 'normal' forms of alienation. The 'normally' alienated person, by reason of the fact that he acts more or less like everyone else, is taken to be sane. Other forms of alienation that are out of step with the prevailing state of alienation are those that are labelled by the 'normal' majority as bad or mad.

The condition of alienation, of being asleep, of being unconscious, of being out of one's mind, is the condition of the normal man.

Society highly values its normal man. It educates children to lose themselves and to become absurd, and thus to be normal.

Normal men have killed perhaps 100,000,000 of their fellow normal men in the last fifty years.

Our behaviour is a function of our experience. We act according to the way we see things.

If our experience is destroyed, our behaviour will be destructive.

If our experience is destroyed, we have lost our own selves.

How much human *behaviour*, whether the interactions between persons themselves or between groups and groups, is intelligible in terms of human *experience*? Either our inter-human behaviour is unintelligible, in that we are simply the passive vehicles of inhuman processes, whose ends are as obscure as they are at present outside our control, or our own behaviour towards each other is a function of our own experience and our own intentions, however alienated we are from them. In the latter case, we must take final responsibility for what we make of what we are made of.

We will find no intelligibility in behaviour if we see it as an inessential phase in an essentially inhuman process. We have had accounts of men as animals, men as machines, men as biochemical complexes with certain ways of their own, but there remains the greatest difficulty in achieving a human understanding of man in human terms.

Men at all times have been subject, as they believed or experienced, to forces from the stars, from the gods, or from forces that now blow through society itself, appearing as the stars once did to determine human fate.

Men have, however, always been weighed down not only by their sense of subordination to fate and chance, to ordained external necessities or contingencies, but by a sense that their very own thoughts and feelings, in their most intimate interstices, are the outcome, the resultant, of processes which they undergo.

A man can estrange himself from himself by mystifying himself and others. He can also have what he does stolen from him by the agency of others.

If we are stripped of experience, we are stripped of our deeds; and if our deeds are, so to say, taken out of our hands like toys from the hands of children, we are bereft of our humanity. We cannot be deceived. Men can and do destroy the humanity of other men, and the condition of this possibility is that we are interdependent. We are not self-contained monads producing no effects on each other except our reflections. We are both acted upon, changed for good or ill, by other men; and we are agents who act upon others to affect them in different ways. Each of us is the other to the others. Man is a patient-agent, agent-patient, interexperiencing and interacting with his fellows.

It is quite certain that unless we can regulate our behaviour much more satisfactorily than at present, then we are going to exterminate ourselves. But as we experience the world, so we act, and this principle holds even when action conceals rather than discloses our experience.

We are not able even to *think* adequately about the behaviour that is at the annihilating edge. But what we think is less than what we know: what we know is less than what we love: what we love is so much less than what there is. And to that precise extent we are so much less than what we are.

Yet if nothing else, each time a new baby is born there is a possibility of reprieve. Each child is a new being, a potential prophet, a new spiritual prince, a new spark of light, precipitated into the outer darkness. Who are we to decide that it is hopeless?

IV. Phantasy as a mode of experience

The 'surface' experience of self and other emerges from a less differentiated experiential matrix. Ontogenetically the very early experiential schemata are unstable, and are surmounted: but never entirely. To a greater or lesser extent, the first ways in which the world has made sense to us continues to underpin our whole subsequent experience and actions. Our first way of experiencing the world is largely what psychoanalysts have called phantasy. This modality has its own validity, its own rationality. Infantile phantasy may become a closed enclave, a dissociated undeveloped 'unconscious', but this need not be so. This eventuality is another form of alienation. Phantasy as encountered in many people today is split off from what the person regards as his mature, sane, rational, adult experience. We do not then see phantasy in its true function but experienced merely as an intrusive, sabotaging infantile nuisance.

For most of our social life, we largely gloss over this underlying phantasy level of our relationship.

Phantasy is a particular way of relating to the world. It is part of, sometimes the essential part of, the meaning or sense (*le sens:* Merleau-Ponty) implicit in action. As relationship we may be dissociated from it: as meaning we may not grasp it: as experience it may escape our notice in different ways. That is, it is possible to speak of phantasy being 'unconscious', if this general statement is always given specific connotations.

However, although phantasy can be unconscious – that is, although we may be unaware of experience in this mode, or refuse to admit that our behaviour implies an experiential relationship or a relational experience that gives it a meaning, often apparent to others if not to ourselves – phantasy need not be thus split from us, whether in terms of its content or modality.

Phantasy, in short, as I am using the term, is always experiential, and meaningful: and, if the person is not dissociated from it, relational in a valid way.

Two people sit talking. The one (Peter) is making a point to the other (Paul). He puts his point of view in different ways to Paul for some time, but Paul does not understand.

Let us *imagine* what may be going on, in the sense that I mean by phantasy. Peter is trying to get through to Paul. He feels that Paul is being needlessly closed up against him. It becomes increasingly important to him to soften, or get into Paul. But Paul seems hard, impervious and cold. Peter feels he is beating his head against a brick wall. He feels tired, hopeless, progressively more empty as he sees he is failing. Finally he gives up.

Paul feels, on the other hand, that Peter is pressing too hard. He feels he has to fight him off. He doesn't understand what Peter is saying, but feels that he has to defend himself from an assault.

The dissociation of each from his phantasy, and the phantasy of the other, betokens the lack of relationship of each to himself and each to the other. They are both more and less related to each other 'in phantasy' than each pretends to be to himself and the other.

Here, two roughly complementary phantasy experiences wildly belie the calm manner in which two men talk to each other, comfortably ensconced in their armchairs.

It is mistaken to regard the above description as merely metaphorical.

V. The negation of experience

There seems to be no agent more effective than another person in bringing a world for oneself alive, or, by a glance, a gesture, or a remark, shrivelling up the reality in which one is lodged.*

The physical environment unremittingly offers us possibilities of experience, or curtails them. The fundamental human significance of architecture stems from this. The glory of Athens, as Pericles so lucidly stated, and the horror of so many features of the modern megalopolis is

* Erving Goffman; *Encounters: Two Studies in the Sociology of Interaction* (Indianapolis: Bobbs-Merrill, 1961) page 41.

that the former enhanced and the latter constricts man's consciousness.

Here however I am concentrating upon what we do to ourselves and to each other.

Let us take the simplest possible interpersonal scheme. Consider Jack and Jill in relation. Then Jack's behaviour towards Jill is experienced by Jill in particular ways. How she experiences him affects considerably how she behaves towards him. How she behaves towards him influences (without by any means totally determining) how he experiences her. And his experience of her contributes to his way of behaving towards her which in turn . . . etc.

Each person may take two fundamentally distinguishable forms of action in this interpersonal system. Each may act on his own experience or upon the other person's experience, *and there is no other form of personal action possible within this system.* That is to say, as long as we are considering personal action of self to self or self to other, the only way one can ever act is on one's own experience or on the other's experience.

Personal action can either open out possibilities of enriched experience or it can shut off possibilities. Personal action is either predominantly validating, confirming, encouraging, supportive, enhancing, or it is invalidating, disconfirming, discouraging, undermining and constricting. It can be creative or destructive.

In a world where the normal condition is one of alienation, most personal action must be destructive both of one's own experience and of that of the other. I shall outline here some of the ways this can be done. I leave the reader to consider from his own experience how pervasive these kinds of action are.

Under the heading of 'defence mechanisms', psychoanalysis describes a number of ways in which a person becomes alienated from himself. For example, repression, denial, splitting, projection, introjection. These 'mechanisms'are often described in psychoanalytic terms as themselves 'unconscious', that is, the person himself appears to be unaware that he is doing this to himself. Even when a person develops sufficient insight to see that 'splitting', for example, is going on, he usually experiences this splitting as indeed a mechanism, so to say, an impersonal process which has taken over, which he can observe but cannot control or stop.

There is thus some phenomenological validity in referring to such 'defences' by the term 'mechanism'. But we must not stop there. They have this mechanical quality, because the person as he experiences himself is dissociated from them. He appears to himself and to others to suffer from them. They seem to be processes he undergoes, and as such he experiences himself as a patient, with a particular psychopathology.

But this is so only from the perspective of his own alienated experience. As he becomes de alienated he is able first of all to become aware of them, if he has not already done so, and then to take the second, even more crucial, step of progressively realizing that these are things he does or has done to himself. Process becomes converted back to praxis, the patient becomes an agent.

Ultimately it is possible to regain the ground that has been lost. These defence mechanisms are actions taken by the person on his own experience. On top of this he has dissociated himself from his own action. The end-product of this twofold violence is a person who no longer experiences himself fully as a person, but as a part of a person, invaded by destructive psychopathological 'mechanisms' in the face of which he is a relatively helpless victim.

These 'defences' are action on oneself. But 'defences' are not only intrapersonal, they are *transpersonal*. I act not only on myself, I can act upon you. And you act not only on yourself, you act upon me. In each case, on *experience*.*

If Jack succeeds in forgetting something, this is of little use if Jill continues to remind him of it. He must induce her not to do so. The safest way would be not just to make her keep quiet about it, but to induce her to forget it also.

Jack may act upon Jill in many ways. He may make her feel guilty for keeping on 'bringing it up'. He may *invalidate* her experience. This can be done more or less radically. He can indicate merely that it is unimportant or trivial, whereas it is important and significant to her. Going further, he can shift the *modality* of her experience from memory to imagination: 'It's all in your imagination.' Further still, he can invalidate the *content*. 'It never happened that way.' Finally, he can invalidate not only the significance, modality and content, but her very capacity to remember at all, and make her feel guilty for doing so into the bargain.

This is not unusual. People are doing such things to each other all the time. In order for such transpersonal invalidation to work, however, it is advisable to overlay it with a thick patina of mystification.† For instance, by denying that this is what one is doing, and further invalidating any perception that it is being done, by ascriptions

* For developments of my theory of *transpersonal* defences, see R. D. Laing, H. Phillipson and A. R. Lee, *Interpersonal Perception: A Theory and a Method of Research* (London: Tavistock Publications, 1966).

† R. D. Laing, 'Mystification, Confusion and Conflict' in *Intensive Family Therapy*, edited by Ivan Bszobrmenyi-Nagy and James L. Framo (New York: Harper & Row, 1965).

such as 'How can you think such a thing?' 'You must be paranoid.' And so on.

VI. The experience of negation

There are many varieties of experience of lack, or absence, and many subtle distinctions between the experience of negation and the negation of experience.

All experience is both active and passive, the unity of the given and the construed; and the construction one places on what is given can be positive or negative: it is what one desires or fears or is prepared to accept, or it is not. The element of negation is in every relationship and every experience of relationship. The distinction between the absence of relationships, and the experience of every relationship as an absence, is the division between loneliness and a perpetual solitude, between provisional hope or hopelessness and a permanent despair. The part I feel I play in generating this state of affairs determines what I feel I can or should do about it.

The first intimations of nonbeing may have been the breast or mother as absent. This seems to have been Freud's suggestion. Winnicott writes of 'the hole', the creation of nothing by devouring the breast. Bion relates the origin of thought to the experience of no-breast. The human being, in Sartre's idiom, does not create being, but rather injects nonbeing into the world, into an original plenitude of being.

Nothing, as experience, arises as absence of someone or something. No friends, no relationships, no pleasure, no meaning in life, no ideas, no mirth, no money. As applied to parts of the body – no breast, no penis, no good or bad contents – emptiness. The list is, in principle, endless. Take anything, and imagine its absence.

PERSONS AND EXPERIENCE

Being and nonbeing is the central theme of all philosophy, East and West. These words are not harmless and innocent verbal arabesques, except in the professional philosophism of decadence.

We are afraid to approach the fathomless and bottomless groundlessness of everything.

'There's nothing to be afraid of.' The ultimate reassurance, and the ultimate terror.

We experience the objects of our experience as *there* in the outside world. The source of our experience seems to be outside ourselves. In the creative experience, we experience the source of the created images, patterns, sounds, to be within ourselves but still beyond ourselves. Colours emanate from a source of pre-light itself unlit, sounds from silence, patterns from formlessness. This pre-formed pre-light, this pre-sound, this pre-form is nothing, and yet it is the source of all created things.

We are separated from and related to one another physically. Persons as embodied beings relate to each other through the medium of space. And we are separated and joined by our different perspectives, educations, backgrounds, organizations, group-loyalties, affiliations, ideologies, socio-economic class interests, temperaments. These social 'things' that unite us are by the same token so many *things*, so many social figments that come between us. But if we could strip away all the exigencies and contingencies, and reveal to each other our naked presence? If you take away everything, all the clothes, the disguises, the crutches, the grease paint, also the common projects, the games that provide the pretexts for the occasions that masquerade as meetings – if we could meet, if there were such a happening, a happy coincidence of human beings, what would now separate us?

33

Two people with first and finally nothing between us. Between us nothing. No thing. That which is really 'between' cannot be named by any things that come between. The between is itself no-thing.

If I draw a pattern on a piece of paper, here is an action I am taking on the ground of my experience of my situation. What do I experience myself as doing and what intention have I? Am I trying to convey something to someone (communication)? Am I rearranging the elements of some internal kaleidoscopic jigsaw (invention)? Am I trying to discover the properties of the new *Gestalten* that emerge (discovery)? Am I amazed that something is appearing that did not exist before? That these lines did not exist on this paper until I put them there? Here we are approaching the *experience* of creation and of nothing.

What is called a poem is compounded perhaps of communication, invention, fecundation, discovery, production, creation. Through all the contention of intentions and motives a miracle has occurred. There is something new under the sun; being has emerged from nonbeing; a spring has bubbled out of a rock.

Without the miracle nothing has happened. Machines are already becoming better at communicating with each other than human beings are with human beings. The situation is ironical. More and more concern about communication, less and less to communicate.

We are not so much concerned with experiences of 'filling a gap' in theory or knowledge, of filling up a hole, of occupying an empty space. It is not a question of putting something *into* nothing, but of the creation of something *out* of nothing. *Ex nihilo*. The no thing out of which the creation emerges, at its purest, is not an empty space, or an empty stretch of time.

At the point of nonbeing we are at the outer reaches of what language can state, but we can indicate by language why language cannot say what it cannot say. I cannot say what cannot be said, but sounds can make us listen to the silence. Within the confines of language it is possible to indicate when the dots must begin.... But in using a word, a letter, a sound, OM, one cannot put a sound to soundlessness, or name the unnameable.

The silence of the preformation expressed in and through language, cannot be expressed by language. But language can be used to convey what it cannot say – by its interstices, by its emptiness and lapses, by the latticework of words, syntax, sound and meanings. The modulations of pitch and volume delineate the form precisely by not filling in the spaces between the lines. But it is a grave mistake to mistake the lines for the pattern, or the pattern for that which it is patterning.

'The sky is blue' suggests that there is a substantive 'sky' that is 'blue'. This sequence of subject verb object, in which 'is' acts as the copula uniting sky and blue, is a nexus of sounds, and syntax, signs and symbols, in which we are fairly completely entangled and which separates us from at the same time as it refers us to that ineffable sky-blue-sky. The sky is blue and blue is *not* sky, sky is not blue. But in saying 'the sky is blue' we say 'the sky' 'is'. The sky exists and it is blue. 'Is' serves to unite everything and at the same time 'is' is not any of the things that it unites.

None of the things that are united by 'is' can themselves qualify 'is'. 'Is' is not this, that, or the next, or anything. Yet 'is' is the condition of the possibility of all things. 'Is' is that no-thing whereby all things are.

'Is' as no-thing, is that whereby all things are. And the

condition of the possibility of anything being at all, is that it is in relation to that which it is not.

That is to say, the ground of the being of all beings is the relation between them. This relationship is the 'is', the being of all things, and the being of all things is itself no-thing. Man creates in transcending himself in revealing himself. But what creates, wherefrom and whereto, the clay, the pot and the potter, are all not-me. I am the witness, the medium, the occasion of a happening that the created thing makes evident.

Man, most fundamentally, is not engaged in the discovery of what is there, nor in production, nor even in communication, nor in invention. He is enabling being to emerge from nonbeing.

The experience of being the actual medium for a continual process of creation takes one past all depression or persecution or vain glory, past, even, chaos or emptiness, into the very mystery of that continual flip of nonbeing into being, and can be the occasion of that great liberation when one makes the transition from being afraid of nothing, to the realization that there is nothing to fear. Nevertheless, it is very easy to lose one's way at any stage, and especially when one is nearest.

Here can be great joy, but it is as easy to be mangled by the process as to swing with it. It will require an act of imagination from those who do not know from their own experience what hell this borderland between being and nonbeing can become. But that is what imagination is for.

One's posture or stance in relation to the act or process can become decisive from the point of view of madness or sanity.

There are men who feel called upon to generate even themselves out of nothing, since their underlying feeling is that they have not been adequately created or have been created only for destruction.

If there are no meanings, no values, no source of sustenance or help, then man, as creator, must invent, conjure up meanings and values, sustenance and succour out of nothing. He is a magician.

A man may indeed produce something new – a poem, a pattern, a sculpture, a system of ideas – think thoughts never before thought, produce sights never before seen. Little benefit is he likely to derive from his own creativity. The phantasy is not modified by such 'acting out', even the sublimest. The fate that awaits the creator, after being ignored, neglected, despised, is, luckily or unluckily according to point of view, to be discovered by the non-creative.

There are sudden, apparently inexplicable suicides that must be understood as the dawn of a hope so horrible and harrowing that it is unendurable.

In our 'normal' alienation from being, the person who has a perilous awareness of the nonbeing of what we take to be being (the pseudo-wants, pseudo-values, pseudo-realities of the endemic delusions of what are taken to be life and death and so on) gives us in our present epoch the acts of creation that we despise and crave.

Words in a poem, sounds in movement, rhythm in space, attempt to recapture personal meaning in personal time and space from out of the sights and sounds of a depersonalized, dehumanized world. They are bridge-heads into alien territory. They are acts of insurrection. Their source is from the Silence at the centre of each of us. Wherever and whenever such a whorl of patterned sound or space is established in the external world, the power that it contains generates new lines of forces whose effects are felt for centuries.

The creative breath 'comes from a zone of man where man cannot descend, even if Virgil were to lead him, for Virgil would not go down there'.*

This zone, the zone of no-thing, of the silence of silences, is the source. We forget that we are all there all the time.

An activity has to be understood in terms of the experience from which it emerges. These arabesques that mysteriously embody mathematical truths only glimpsed by a very few – how beautiful, how exquisite – no matter that they were the threshing and thrashing of a drowning man.

We are here beyond all questions except those of being and nonbeing, incarnation, birth, life and death.

Creation *ex nihilo* has been pronounced impossible even for God. But we are concerned with miracles. We must hear the music of those Braque guitars (Lorca).

From the point of view of a man alienated from his source creation arises from despair and ends in failure. But such a man has not trodden the path to the end of time, the end of space, the end of darkness, and the end of light. He does not know that where it all ends, there it all begins.

* *The Journals of Jean Cocteau,* translated by Wallace Fowlie (Bloomington: Indiana University Press 1964).

Chapter 2

The Psychotherapeutic Experience*

IN the last twenty years, psychotherapy has developed both in theory and in practice in complex ways. And yet, through all this tangled complexity and sometimes confusion, it is impossible, in the words of Pasternak, 'not to fall ultimately, as into a heresy, into unheard of simplicity'.

In the practice of psychotherapy, the very diversities of method have made the essential simplicity more clear.

The irreducible elements of psychotherapy are a therapist, a patient, and a regular and reliable time and place. But given these, it is not so easy for two people to meet. We all live on the hope that authentic meeting between human beings can still occur. Psychotherapy consists in the paring away of all that stands between us, the props, masks, roles, lies, defences, anxieties, projections and introjections, in short, all the carry-overs from the past, transference and counter-transference, that we use by habit and collusion, wittingly or unwittingly, as our currency for relationships. It is this currency, these very media, that re-create and intensify the conditions of alienation that originally occasioned them.

The distinctive contribution of psychoanalysis has been to bring to light these importations, carry-overs, compulsive repetitions. The tendency now, among pyschoanalysts and psychotherapists is to focus not only on transference, not only on what has happened before, but on what has never happened before, on what is new. Thus, in practice, the use of interpretations to reveal the past, or even to reveal the past-in-the-present, may be used as

* From the point of view of the psychotherapist.

only one tactic and, in theory, there are efforts to understand better and to find words for the *non*-transference elements in psychotherapy.

The therapist may allow himself to act spontaneously and unpredictably. He may set out actively to disrupt old patterns of experience and behaviour. He may actively reinforce new ones. One hears now of therapists giving orders, laughing, shouting, crying, even getting up from that sacred chair. Zen, with its emphasis on illumination achieved through the sudden and unexpected, is a growing influence. Of course such techniques in the hands of a man who has not unremitting concern and respect for the patient could be disastrous. Although some general principles of these developments can be laid down, their practice is still, and indeed must always be, for the man who has both quite exceptional authority and the capacity to improvise.

I shall not enumerate all the many practical varieties of psychotherapy, long and short, brief, intensive, experiential, directive and non-directive, those that utilize the conscious-expanding drugs or other adjuvants, and those that use, as it were, nothing but persons. I wish rather to consider in more detail the critical function of theory.

These lines of growth that seem to expand centrifugally in all directions have intensified the need for a strong, firm primary theory that can draw each practice and theory into relation to the central concerns of all forms of psychotherapy. In the last chapter I outlined some of the fundamental requirements of such a theory. Namely, that we need concepts which both indicate the interaction and interexperience of two persons, and help us to understand the relation between each person's own experience and his own behaviour, within the context of the relationship between them. And we must in turn be able to conceive of this relationship within the relevant contextual social *systems*. Most fundamentally a critical theory must be able to place all theories and practices within the scope of a total vision of the ontological structure of being human.

What help are the prevailing theories of psychotherapy to us? Here it would be misleading to delineate too sharply one school of thought from another. Within the mainstream of orthodox psychoanalysis and even between the different theories of object-relationships in the U.K. – Fairbairn, Winnicott, Melanie Klein, Bion – there are differences of more than emphasis: similarly within the Existential school or tradition – Binswanger, Boss, Caruso, Frankl. Every theoretical idiom could be found to play some part in the thinking of at least some members of any school. At worst there are the most extraordinary theoretical mixes of learning theory, ethology, system theory, communications analysis, information theory, transactional analysis, interpersonal relations, object relations, games theory, and so on.

Freud's development of metapsychology changed the theoretical context we now work in. To understand with sympathy the positive value of metapsychology, we have to consider the intellectual climate in which it was first developed. Others have pointed out that it drew its impetus from the attempt to see man as an object of natural scientific investigation, and thus to win acceptance for psychoanalysis as a serious and respectable enterprise. I do not think such a shield is now necessary; or even, that it ever was. And the price paid when one thinks in metapsychological terms is high.

The metapsychology of Freud, Federn, Rapaport, Hartman, Kris, has no constructs for any social system generated by more than one person at a time. Within its

41

own framework it has no concepts of social collectivities of experience shared or unshared between persons. This theory has no category of 'you', as there is in the work of Feuerbach, Buber, Parsons. It has no way of expressing the meeting of an 'I' with 'an other', and of the impact of one person on another. It has no concept of 'me' except as objectified as 'the ego'. The ego is one part of a mental apparatus. Internal objects are other parts of this system. Another ego is part of a different system or structure. How two mental apparatuses or psychic structures or systems, each with its own constellation of internal objects, can relate to each other remains unexamined. Within the constructs the theory offers, it is possibly inconceivable. Projection and introjection do not in themselves bridge the gap *between* persons.

Few now find central the issues of conscious and unconscious as conceived by the early psychoanalysts – as two reified systems, both split from the totality of the person, both composed of some sort of psychic stuff, and both exclusively *intra*personal.

It is the relation *between persons* that is central in theory, and in practice. Persons are related to one another through their experience and through their behaviour. Theories can be seen in terms of the emphasis they put on *experience* or on *behaviour*, and in terms of their ability to articulate the relationship between experience and behaviour.

The different schools of psychoanalysis and depth psychology have at least recognized the crucial relevance of each person's experience to his or her behaviour, but they have left unclarified what *is* experience, and this is particularly evident in respect of 'the unconscious'.

Some theories are more concerned with the interactions

or transactions between people, without too much reference to the experience of the agents. Just as any theory that focuses on *experience* and neglects behaviour can become very misleading, so theories that focus on behaviour to the neglect of experience become unbalanced.

In the idiom of games theory, people have a repertoire of games, based on particular sets of learned interactions. Others may play games that mesh sufficiently to allow a variety of more or less stereotyped dramas to be enacted. The games have rules, some public, some secret. Some people play games that break the rules of games that others play. Some play undeclared games, so rendering their moves ambiguous or downright unintelligible, except to the expert in such secret and unusual games. Such people, prospective neurotics or psychotics, may have to undergo the ceremonial of a psychiatric consultation, leading to diagnosis, prognosis, prescription. Treatment would consist in pointing out to them the unsatisfactory nature of the games they play and perhaps teaching new games. A person reacts by despair more to loss of the *game* than to sheer 'object-loss', that is, to the loss of his partner or partners as real persons. The maintenance of the game rather than the identity of players is all important.

One advantage of this idiom is that it relates persons together. The failure to see the behaviour of one person in relation to the behaviour of the other has led to much confusion. In a sequence of an interaction between p and o, $p_1 \rightarrow o_1 \rightarrow p_2 \rightarrow o_2 \rightarrow p_3 \rightarrow o_3$, etc., p's contribution p_1, p_2, to p_3 is taken out of context and direct links are made between $p_1 \rightarrow p_1 \rightarrow p_3$. This artificially derived sequence is then studied as an isolated entity or process and attempts may be made to 'explain' it (find the

'aetiology') in terms of genetic-constitutional factors or
intra-psychic pathology.

Object-relations theory attempts to achieve, as Gun-
trip has argued, a synthesis between the intra and inter
personal. Its concepts of internal and external objects, of
closed and open systems, go some way. Yet it is still
objects not persons that are in question. Objects are the
what not the whereby of experience. The brain is itself an
object of experience. We still require a phenomenology of
experience including so-called unconscious experience, of
experience related to behaviour, of person related to
person, without splitting, denial, depersonalization, and
reification, all fruitless attempts to explain the whole by
the part.

Transaction, systems, games, can occur and can be
played in and between electronic systems. What is
specifically personal or human? A personal relationship is
not only transactional, it is transexperiential and herein is
its specific human quality. Transaction alone without
experience lacks specific personal connotations. Endo-
crine and reticuloendothelial systems transact. They are
not persons. The great danger of thinking about man
by means of analogy is that the analogy comes to be put
forward as a homology.

Why do almost all theories about depersonalization,
reification, splitting, denial, tend themselves to exhibit the
symptoms they attempt to describe? We are left with,
transactions, but where is the individual? the individual,
but where is the other? patterns of behaviour, but where
is the experience? information and communication, but
where is the pathos and sympathy, the passion and compassion?

Behaviour therapy is the most extreme example of such
schizoid theory and practice that proposes to think and

act purely in terms of the other, without reference to the self of the therapist or the patient, in terms of behaviour without experience, in terms of objects rather than persons. It is inevitably therefore a technique of non-meeting, of manipulation and control.

Psychotherapy must remain *an obstinate attempt of two people to recover the wholeness of being human through the relationship between them.*

Any technique concerned with the other without the self, with behaviour to the exclusion of experience, with the relationship to the neglect of the persons in relation, with the individuals to the exclusion of their relationship, and most of all, with an object-to-be-changed rather than a person-to-be-accepted, simply perpetuates the disease it purports to cure.

And any *theory* not founded on the nature of being human is a lie and a betrayal of man. An inhuman theory will inevitably lead to inhuman consequences – if the therapist is consistent. Fortunately, many therapists have the gift of inconsistency. This, however endearing, cannot be regarded as ideal.

We are not concerned with the interaction of two objects, nor with their transactions within a dyadic system; we are not concerned with the communication patterns within a system comprising two computer-like sub-systems that receive and process input, and emit outgoing signals. Our concern is with two origins of experience in relation.

Behaviour can conceal or disclose experience. I devoted a book, *The Divided Self*,* to describing some versions of the split between experience and behaviour. And both experience and behaviour are themselves fragmented in a myriad different ways. This is so even when enormous

* London: Tavistock Publications, 1960; Penguin Books, 1965.

efforts are made to apply a veneer of consistency over the cracks.

I suggest the reason for this confusion lies in the meaning of Heidegger's phrase, *the Dreadful has already happened.*

Psychotherapists are specialists, in human relations. But the Dreadful has already happened. It has happened to us all. The therapists, too, are in a world in which the inner is already split from the outer. The inner does not become outer, and the outer become inner, just by the re-discovery of the 'inner' world. That is only the beginning. As a whole generation of men, we are so estranged from the inner world that there are many arguing that it does not exist; and that even if it does exist, it does not matter. Even if it has some significance, it is not the hard stuff of science, and if it is not, then let's make it hard. Let it be measured and counted. Quantify the heart's agony and ecstasy in a world in which, when the inner world is first discovered, we are liable to find ourselves bereft and derelict. For without the inner the outer loses its meaning and without the outer the inner loses its substance.

We must know about relations and communications. But these disturbed and disturbing patterns of communication reflect the disarray of personal worlds of experience whose repression, denial, splitting, introjection, projection, etc. – whose general desecration and profanation our civilization is based upon.

When our personal worlds are rediscovered and allowed to reconstitute themselves, we first discover a shambles. Bodies half-dead; genitals dissociated from heart; heart severed from head; heads dissociated from genitals. Without inner unity, with just enough sense of continuity to clutch at identity – the current idolatry. Torn, body, mind and spirit, by inner contradictions, pulled in different directions, Man cut off from his own mind, cut off equally from his own body – a half-crazed creature in a mad world.

When the Dreadful has already happened, we can hardly expect other than that the Thing will echo externally the destruction already wrought internally.

We are all implicated in this state of affairs of alienation. This context is decisive for the whole practice of psychotherapy.

The psychotherapeutic relationship is therefore a research. A search, constantly reasserted and reconstituted for what we have all lost, and which some can perhaps endure a little more easily than others, as some people can stand lack of oxygen better than others, and *this re-search is validated by the shared experience of experience regained in and through the therapeutic relationship in the here and now.*

True, in the enterprise of psychotherapy there are regularities, even institutional structures, pervading the sequence, rhythm and tempo of the therapeutic situation viewed as process, and these can and should be studied with scientific objectivity. But the really decisive moments in psychotherapy, as every patient or therapist who has ever experienced them knows, are unpredictable, unique, unforgettable, always unrepeatable, and often indescribable. Does this mean that psychotherapy must be a pseudo-esoteric cult? No.

We must continue to struggle through our confusion, to nsist on being human.

Existence is a flame which constantly melts and recasts our theories. Existential thinking offers no security, no home for the homeless. It addresses no one except you and me. It finds its validation when, across the gulf of our idioms and styles, our mistakes, errings, and perversities,

47

we find in the other's communication an experience of relationship established, lost, destroyed, or regained. We hope to share the experience of a relationship, but the only honest beginning, or even end, may be to share the experience of its absence.

Chapter 3

The Mystification of Experience

IT is not enough to destroy one's own and other people's experience. One must overlay this devastation by a false consciousness inured, as Marcuse puts it, to its own falsity.

Exploitation must not be seen as such. It must be seen as benevolence. Persecution preferably should not need to be invalidated as the figment of a paranoid imagination, it should be experienced as kindness. Marx described mystification and showed its function in his day. Orwell's time is already with us. The colonists not only mystify the natives, in the ways that Fanon so clearly shows,* they have to mystify themselves. We in Europe and North America are the colonists, and in order to sustain our amazing images of ourselves as God's gift to the vast majority of the starving human species, we have to interiorize our violence upon ourselves and our children and to employ the rhetoric of morality to describe this process.

In order to rationalize our industrial-military complex, we have to destroy our capacity both to see clearly any more what is in front of, and to imagine what is beyond, our noses. Long before a thermonuclear war can come about, we have had to lay waste our own sanity. We begin with the children. It is imperative to catch them in time. Without the most thorough and rapid brain-washing their dirty minds would see through our dirty tricks. Children are not yet fools, but we shall turn them into imbeciles like ourselves, with high I.Q.s if possible.

* Frantz Fanon, *The Wretched of the Earth* (London: MacGibbon and Kee, 1965); also Frantz Fanon, *Studies in a Dying Colonialism* (New York: Monthly Review Press, 1965).

From the moment of birth, when the stone-age baby confronts the twentieth-century mother, the baby is subjected to these forces of violence, called love, as its mother and father have been, and their parents and their parents before them. These forces are mainly concerned with destroying most of its potentialities. This enterprise is on the whole successful. By the time the new human being is fifteen or so, we are left with a being like ourselves. A half-crazed creature, more or less adjusted to a mad world. This is normality in our present age.

Love and violence, properly speaking, are polar opposites. Love lets the other be, but with affection and concern. Violence attempts to constrain the other's freedom, to force him to act in the way we desire, but with ultimate lack of concern, with indifference to the other's own existence of destiny.

We are effectively destroying ourselves by violence masquerading as love.

I am a specialist, God help me, in events in inner space and time, in experiences called thoughts, images, reveries, memories, dreams, visions, hallucinations, dreams of memories, memories of dreams, memories of visions, dreams of hallucinations, refractions of refractions of refractions of that original Alpha and Omega of experience and reality, that Reality on whose repression, denial, splitting, projection, falsification, and general desecration and profanation our civilization as much as on anything is based.

We live equally out of our bodies, and out of our minds.

Concerned as I am with this inner world, observing day in and day out its devastation, I ask why this has happened?

One component of an answer suggested in Chapter 1, is that we can *act* on our *experience* of ourselves, others and the world, as well as take action on the world through behaviour itself. Specifically this devastation is largely the work of *violence* that has been perpetrated on each of us, and by each of us on ourselves. The usual name that much of this violence goes under is *love*.

We act on our experience at the behest of the others, just as we learn how to behave in compliance to them. We are taught what to experience and what not to experience, as we are taught what movements to make and what sounds to emit. A child of two is already a moral mover and moral talker and moral experiencer. He already moves the 'right' way, makes the 'right' noises, and knows what he should feel and what he should not feel. His movements have become stereometric types, enabling the specialist anthropologist to identify, through his rhythm and style, his national, even his regional, characteristics. As he is taught to move in specific ways, out of the whole range of possible movements, so he is taught to experience, out of the whole range of possible experience.

Much current social science deepens the mystification. Violence cannot be seen through the sights of positivism.

A woman grinds stuff down a goose's neck through a funnel. Is this a description of cruelty to an animal? She disclaims any motivation or intention of cruelty. If we were to describe this scene 'objectively' we would only be denuding it of what is 'objectively' or, better, ontologically present in the situation. Every description presupposes our ontological premises as to the nature (being) of man, of animals, and of the relationship between them.

If an animal is debased to a manufactured piece of produce, a sort of biochemical complex – so that its flesh and organs are simply material that has a certain texture in the mouth (soft, tender, tough), a taste, perhaps a smell – then to describe the animal *positively* in those terms is to debase oneself by debasing being itself. A *positive* description is not 'neutral' or 'objective'. In the case of geese-as-raw-material-for-*pâté*, one can only give a negative description if the description is to remain underpinned by a valid ontology. That is to say, the description moves in the light of what this activity is a brutalization of, a debasement of, a desecration of: namely, the true nature of human beings and of animals.

The description must be *in the light of* the fact that the human beings have become so self-brutalized, banalized, stultified, that they are unaware of their own debasement. This is not to superimpose on to the 'neutral' description certain value-judgements that have lost all criterion of 'objective' validity, that is to say, any validity that anyone feels needs to be taken really seriously. On 'subjective' matters, anything goes. Political ideologies, on the other hand, are riddled with value-judgements, unrecognized as such, that have no ontological validity. Pedants teach youth that such questions of value are unanswerable, or untestable, or unverifiable, or not really questions at all, or that what we require are meta-questions. Meanwhile Vietnam goes on.

Under the sign of alienation every single aspect of the human reality is subject to falsification, and a positive description can only perpetuate the alienation which it cannot itself describe, and succeeds only in further deepening it, because it disguises and masks it the more.

We must then repudiate a positivism that achieves its 'reliability' by a successful masking of what is and what is not, by a serialization of the world of the observer by turning the truly given into *capta* which are *taken as given*, by the denuding of the world of being and relegating the ghost of being to a shadow land of subjective 'values'.

The theoretical and descriptive idiom of much research in social science adopts a stance of apparent 'objective' neutrality. But we have seen how deceptive this can be. The choice of syntax and vocabulary are political acts that define and circumscribe the manner in which 'facts' are to be experienced. Indeed, in a sense they go further and even create the facts that are studied.

The 'data' (given) of research are not so much given as *taken* out of a constantly elusive matrix of happenings. We should speak of *capta* rather than data. The quantitatively interchangeable grist that goes into the mills of reliability studies and rating scales is the expression of a processing that we do *on* reality, which is not the expression of the processes *of* reality.

Natural scientific investigations are conducted on objects, or things, or the patterns of relations between things, or on systems of 'events'. Persons are distinguished from things in that persons experience the world, whereas things behave in the world. Thing-events do not experience. Personal events are experiential. Natural scientism is the error of turning persons into things by a process of reification that is not itself part of the true natural scientific method. Results derived in this way have to be dequantified and dereified before they can be reassimilated into the realm of human discourse.

The error fundamentally is the failure to realize that there is an ontological discontinuity between human beings and it-beings.

Human beings relate to each other not simply externally, like two billiard balls, but by the relations of the two worlds of experience that come into play when two people meet.

If human beings are not studied as human beings, then this once more is violence and mystification.

In much contemporary writing on the individual and the family there is the assumption that there is some not-too-unhappy confluence, not to say pre-established harmony, between nature and nurture. There may be some adjustments to be made on both sides, but all things work together for good to those who want only security and identity.

Gone is any sense of possible tragedy, of passion. Gone is any language of joy, delight, passion, sex, violence. The language is that of a boardroom. No more primal scenes, but parental coalitions; no more repression of sexual ties to parents, but the child 'rescinds' its Oedipal wishes. For instance:

The mother can properly invest her energies in the care of the young child when economic support, status, and protection of the family are provided by the father. She can also better limit her cathexis of the child to maternal feelings when her wifely needs are satisfied by her husband.*

Here is no nasty talk of sexual intercourse or even 'primal scene'. The economic metaphor is aptly employed. The mother 'invests' in her child. What is most revealing is the husband's function. The provision of economic support, status, and protection, in that order.

There is frequently reference to security, the esteem of others. What one is supposed to want, to live for, is 'gaining pleasure from the esteem and affection of others'.† If not, one is a psychopath.

Such statements are in a sense true. They describe the frightened, cowed, abject creature that we are admonished to be, if we are to be normal – offering each

* T. Lidz, *The Family and Human Adaptation* (London: Hogarth Press, 1964) page 54.

† Ibid., page 34.

other mutual protection from our own violence. The family as a 'protection racket'.

Behind this language lurks the terror that is behind all this mutual back-scratching, this esteem-, status-, support-, protection-, security-giving and getting. Through its bland urbanity the cracks still show.

In our world we are 'victims burning at the stake, signalling through the flames', but to Lidz *et al.* things go blandly on. 'Contemporary life requires adaptability.' We require also to 'utilize intellect' and we require 'an emotional equilibrium that permits a person to be malleable, to adjust himself to others without fear of loss of identity with change. It requires a basic trust in others, and a confidence in the integrity of the self.'*

Sometimes there is a glimpse of more honesty. For instance, when we 'consider society rather than the individual, each society has a vital interest in the *indoctrination* of the infants who form its new *recruits*'.†

What these authors say may be written ironically, but there is no evidence that it is.

Adaptation to what? To society? To a world gone mad?

The Family's function is to repress Eros: to induce a false consciousness of security: to deny death by avoiding life: to cut off transcendence: to believe in God, not to experience the Void: to create, in short, one-dimensional man: to promote respect, conformity, obedience: to con children out of play: to induce a fear of failure: to promote a respect for work: to promote a respect for 're-spectability'.

Let me present here two alternative views of the family and human adaptation:

Men do not become what by nature they are meant to be, but what society makes them. . . . generous feelings . . . are, as

* Ibid., pages 28–9.   † Ibid., page 19.

it were, shrunk up, seared, violently wrenched, and amputated to fit us for our intercourse with the world, something in the manner that beggars maim and mutilate their children to make them fit for their future situation in life.*

and:

In fact, the world still seems to be inhabited by savages stupid enough to see reincarnated ancestors in their newborn children. Weapons and jewelry belonging to the dead man are waved under the infant's nose; if he makes a movement, there is a great shout – Grandfather has come back to life. This 'old man' will suckle, dirty his straw and bear the ancestral name; survivors of his ancient generation will enjoy seeing their comrade of hunts and battles wave his tiny limbs and bawl; as soon as he can speak they will inculcate recollections of the deceased. A severe training will 'restore' his former character, they will remind him that 'he' was wrathful, cruel or magnanimous, and he will be convinced of it despite all experience to the contrary. What barbarism! Take a living child, sew him up in a dead man's skin, and he will stifle in such senile childhood with no occupation save to reproduce the avuncular gestures, with no hope save to poison future childhoods after his own death. No wonder, after that, if he speaks of himself with the greatest precautions, half under his breath, often in the third person; this miserable creature is well aware that he is his own grandfather.

These backward aborigines can be found in the Fiji Islands, in Tahiti, in New Guinea, in Vienna, in Paris, in Rome, in New York – wherever there are men. They are called parents. Long before our birth, even before we are conceived, our parents have decided who we will be.†

* E. Colby, (ed.) *The Life of Thomas Holcroft, continued by William Hazlitt* (London: Constable & Co., 1925) Volume II, page 82.

† J. P. Sartre, Foreword to *The Traitor* by André Gorz (London: Calder, 1960) pages 14–15.

In some quarters there is a point of view that science is neutral, and that all this is a matter of value-judgements.

Lidz calls schizophrenia a failure of human adaptation. In that case, this too is a value-judgement. Or is anyone going to say that this is an objective fact? Very well, let us call schizophrenia a successful attempt not to adapt to pseudo social realities. Is this also an objective fact? Schizophrenia is a failure of ego functioning. Is this a neutralist definition? But what is, or who is, the 'ego'? In order to get back to what the ego is, to what actual reality it most nearly relates to, we have to desegregate it, de-depersonalize it, de-extrapolate, de-abstract, de-objectify, de-reify, and we get back to you and me, to our particular idioms or styles of relating to each other in social context. The ego is by definition an instrument of adaptation, so we are back to all the questions this apparent neutralism is begging. Schizophrenia is a successful avoidance of ego-type adaptation? Schizophrenia is a label affixed by some people to others in situations where an interpersonal disjunction of a particular kind is occurring. This is the nearest one can get at the moment to something like an 'objective' statement, so called.

The family is, in the first place, the usual instrument for what is called socialization, that is, getting each new recruit to the human race to behave and experience in substantially the same way as those who have already got here. We are all fallen Sons of Prophecy, who have learned to die in the Spirit and be reborn in the flesh.

This is known also as selling one's birthright for a mess of pottage.

Here are some examples from Jules Henry, an American professor of anthropology and sociology, in his study of the American school system:

The observer is just entering her fifth-grade classroom for the observation period. The teacher says, 'Which one of you nice, polite boys would like to take (the observer's) coat and hang it up?' From the waving hands, it would seem that all would like to claim the honor. The teacher chooses one child, who takes the observer's coat. . . . The teacher conducted the arithmetic lessons mostly by asking, 'Who would like to tell the answer to the next problem?' This question was followed by the usual large and agitated forest of hands, with apparently much competition to answer.

What strikes us here are the precision with which the teacher was able to mobilize the potentialities of the boys for the proper social behaviour, and the speed with which they responded. The large number of waving hands proves that most of the boys have already become absurd; but they have no choice. Suppose they sat there frozen?

A skilled teacher sets up many situations in such a way that a *negative attitude can be construed only as treason.* The function of questions like, 'Which one of you nice, polite boys would like to take (the observer's) coat and hang it up?' is to blind the children into absurdity – to compel them to acknowledge that absurdity is existence, to acknowledge that it is better to exist absurd than not to exist at all. The reader will have observed that the question is not put, 'Who *has* the answer to the next problem?' but 'Who *would like to tell* it?' What at one time in our culture was phrased as a challenge in skill in arithmetic, becomes an invitation to group participation. The essential issue is *that nothing is but what it is made to be by the alchemy of the system.*

In a society where competition for the basic cultural goods is a pivot of action, people cannot be taught to love one another. It thus becomes necessary for the school to teach children how to hate, and without appearing to do so, for our culture cannot tolerate the idea that babes should hate each other. How does the school accomplish this ambiguity?*

* J. Henry, *Culture Against Man* (New York: Random House, 1963) page 293.

Here is another example given by Henry:

Boris had trouble reducing 12/16 to the lowest terms, and could only get as far as 6/8. The teacher asked him quietly if that was as far as he could reduce it. She suggested he 'think'. Much heaving up and down and waving of hands by the other children, all frantic to correct him. Boris pretty unhappy, probably mentally paralysed. The teacher quiet, patient, ignores the others and concentrates with look and voice on Boris. After a minute or two she turns to the class and says, 'Well, who can tell Boris what the number is?' A forest of hands appears, and the teacher calls Peggy. Peggy says that four may be divided into the numerator and the denominator.*

Henry comments:

Boris's failure made it possible for Peggy to succeed; his misery is the occasion for her rejoicing. This is a standard condition of the contemporary American elementary school. To a Zuni, Hopi or Dakota Indian, Peggy's performance would seem cruel beyond belief, for competition, the wringing of success from somebody's failure, is a form of torture foreign to those non-competitive cultures.

Looked at from Boris's point of view, the nightmare at the blackboard was, perhaps, a lesson in controlling himself so that he would not fly shrieking from the room under enormous public pressure. Such experiences force every man reared in our culture, over and over again, night in, night out, even at the pinnacle of success, to dream not of success, but of failure. In school the external nightmare is internalized for life. Boris was not learning arithmetic only; he was learning the *essential nightmare also. To be successful in our culture one must learn to dream of failure.*†

It is Henry's contention that education in practice has never been an instrument to free the mind and the spirit

---

* Ibid., page 27.   † Ibid., pages 295–6.

of man, but to bind them. We think we want creative children, but what do we want them to create?

If all through school the young were provoked to question the Ten Commandments, the sanctity of revealed religion, the foundations of patriotism, the profit motive, the two-party system, monogamy, the laws of incest, and so on . . .*

. . . there would be such creativity that society would not know where to turn.

Children do not give up their innate imagination, curiosity, dreaminess easily. You have to love them to get them to do that. Love is the path through permissiveness to discipline: and through discipline, only too often, to betrayal of self.

What school must do is to induce children to want to think the way school wants them to think. 'What we see', in the American kindergarten and early schooling process, says Henry, 'is the pathetic surrender of babies.' You will I trust recognize the principles whether they are applied later or sooner, in the school or in the home.

It is the most difficult thing in the world to see this sort of thing in our own culture.

In a London class, average age ten, the girls were given a competition. They had to bake cakes and the boys were to judge them. One girl won. Then her 'friend' let out that she had bought her cake instead of baking it herself. She was disgraced in front of the whole class.

Comments:

1. The school is here inducting children into sex-linked roles of a very specific kind.

2. Personally, I find it obscene that girls should be taught that their status depends on the taste they can produce in boys' mouths.

* Ibid., page 288.

3. Ethical values are brought into play in a situation that is at best a bad joke. If one is coerced into such game-playing by adults, the best a child can do is to play the system without getting caught. I most admire the girl who won, and hope she will choose her 'friends' more carefully in future.

What Henry describes in American schools is a strategy that I have observed frequently in British families studied by my colleagues and myself.

The double action of destroying ourselves with one hand, and calling this love with the other, is a sleight of hand one can marvel at. Human beings seem to have an almost unlimited capacity to deceive themselves, and to deceive themselves into taking their own lies for truth. By such mystification, we achieve and sustain our adjustment, adaptation, socialization. But the result of such adjustment to our society is that, having been tricked and having tricked ourselves out of our minds, that is to say, out of our own personal world of experience, out of that unique meaning with which potentially we may endow the external world, simultaneously we have been conned into the illusion that we are separate 'skin-encapsuled egos'. Having at one and the same time lost our *selves*, and developed the illusion that we are autonomous *egos*, we are expected to comply by inner consent with external constraints, to an almost unbelievable extent.

We do not live in a world of unambiguous identities and definitions, needs and fears, hopes, disillusions. The tremendous social realities of our time are ghosts, spectres of the murdered gods and our own humanity returned to haunt and destroy us. The Negroes, the Jews, the Reds. *Them.* Only you and me dressed differently. The texture of the fabric of these socially shared hallucinations is what we call reality, and our collusive madness is what we call sanity.

Let no one suppose that this madness exists only somewhere in the night or day sky where our birds of death hover in the stratosphere. It exists in the interstices of our most intimate and personal moments.

We have all been processed on Procrustean beds. At least some of us have managed to hate what they have made of us. Inevitably we see the other as the reflection of the occasion of our own self-division.

The others have become installed in our hearts, and we call them ourselves. Each person, not being himself either to himself or the other, just as the other is not himself to himself or to us, in being another for another neither recognizes himself in the other, nor the other in himself. Hence being at least a double absence, haunted by the ghost of his own murdered self, no wonder modern man is addicted to other persons, and the more addicted, the less satisfied, the more lonely.

Once more there is a further turn of the spiral, another round of the vicious circle, another twist of the tourniquet. For now love becomes a further alienation, a further act of violence. My need is a need to be needed, my longing a longing to be longed for. I act now to install what I take to be myself in what I take to be the other person's heart. Marcel Proust wrote:

How have we the courage to wish to live, how can we make a movement to preserve ourselves from death, in a world where love is provoked by a lie and consists solely in the need of having our sufferings appeased by whatever being has made us suffer?

But no one makes us suffer. The violence we perpetrate and have done to us, the recriminations, reconciliations, the ecstasies and the agonies of a love affair, are based on the socially conditioned illusion that two actual persons are in relationship. Under the circumstances, this is a dangerous state of hallucination and delusion, a mish-mash of phantasy, exploding and imploding, of broken hearts, reparation and revenge.

Yet within all this, I do not preclude the occasions when, most lost, lovers may discover each other, moments when recognition does occur, when hell can turn to heaven and come down to earth, when this crazy distraction can become joy and celebration.

And, at the very least, it befits Babes in the Wood to be kinder to each other, to show some sympathy and compassion, if there is any pathos and passion left to spend.

But when violence masquerades as love, once the fissure into self and ego, inner and outer, good and bad occurs, all else is an infernal dance of false dualities. It has always been recognized that if you split Being down the middle, if you insist on grabbing *this* without *that*, if you cling to the good without the bad, denying the one for the other, what happens is that the dissociated evil impulse, now evil in a double sense, returns to permeate and possess the good and turn it into itself.

When the great Tao is lost, spring forth benevolence and righteousness.

When wisdom and sagacity arise, there are great hypocrites.

When family relations are no longer harmonious, we have filial children and devoted parents.

When a nation is in confusion and disorder, patriots are recognized.

We must be very careful of our selective blindness. The Germans reared children to regard it as their duty to exterminate the Jews, adore their leader, to kill and die for the Fatherland. The majority of my own generation did not or do not regard it as stark raving mad to feel it better to be dead than Red. None of us, I take it, has lost too many hours' sleep over the threat of imminent annihilation of the human race and our own responsibility for this state of affairs.

In the last fifty years, we human beings have slaughtered by our own hands coming on for one hundred million of our species. We all live under constant threat of our total annihilation. We seem to seek death and destruction as much as life and happiness. We are as driven to kill and be killed as we are to let live and live. Only by the most outrageous violation of ourselves have we achieved our capacity to live in relative adjustment to a civilization apparently driven to its own destruction. Perhaps to a limited extent we can undo what has been done to us, and what we have done to ourselves. Perhaps men and women were born to love one another, simply and genuinely, rather than to this travesty that we can call love. If we can stop destroying ourselves we may stop destroying others. We have to begin by admitting and even accepting our violence, rather than blindly destroying ourselves with it, and therewith we have to realize that we are as deeply afraid to live and to love as we are to die.

Chapter 4

Us and Them

ONLY when something has become problematic do we start to ask questions. Disagreement shakes us out of our slumbers, and forces us to see our own point of view through contrast with another person who does not share it. But we resist such confrontations. The history of heresies of all kinds testifies to more than the tendency to break off communication (excommunication) with those who hold different dogmas or opinions; it bears witness to our intolerance of different *fundamental structures of experience*. We seem to need to share a communal meaning to human existence, to give with others a common sense to the world, to maintain a *consensus*.

But it seems that once certain fundamental structures of experience are shared, they come to be experienced as objective entities. These reified projections of our own freedom are then introjected. By the time the sociologists study these projected-introjected reifications, they have taken on the appearance of things. They are not things ontologically. But they are pseudo-things. Thus far Durkheim was quite right to emphasize that collective representations come to be experienced as things, exterior to anyone. They take on the force and character of partial autonomous realities, with their own way of life. A social norm may come to impose an oppressive obligation on everyone, although few people feel it to be their own.

At this moment in history, we are all caught in the hell of frenetic passivity. We find ourselves threatened by extermination that will be reciprocal, that no one wishes, that everyone fears, that may just happen to us 'because' no one knows how to stop it. There is one possibility of doing so if we can understand the structure of this alienation of ourselves from our experience, our experience from our deeds, our deeds from human authorship. Everyone will be carrying out orders. Where do they come from? Always from elsewhere. Is it still possible to reconstitute our destiny out of this hellish and inhuman fatality?

Within this most vicious circle, we obey and defend beings that exist only in so far as we continue to invent and to perpetuate them. What ontological status have these group beings?

This human scene is a scene of mirages, demonic pseudo-realities, because everyone believes everyone else believes them.

How can we find our way back to ourselves again? Let us begin by trying to think about it.

We act not only in terms of our own experience, but of what we think *they* experience, and how we think they think we experience, and so on in a logically vertiginous spiral to infinity.*

Our language is only partially adequate to express this state of affairs. On level 1, two people, or two groups, may agree or disagree. As we say, they see eye to eye or otherwise. They share a common point of view. But on level 2 they may or may not think they agree or disagree, and they may or may not be correct in either case.

* Elsewhere I have worked out a schema to try to think about some of these issues. This is based on theories of a number of thinkers, notably Durkheim, Sartre, Husserl, Schultz, Mead and Dewey. See R. D. Laing, H. Phillipson and A. R. Lee, *Interpersonal Perception: A Theory and a Method of Research* (London: Tavistock Publications, 1966; New York: Springer 1966).

Whereas level 1 is concerned with agreement or disagreement, level 2 is concerned with understanding or misunderstanding. Level 3 is concerned with a third level of awareness: what do I think you think I think? That is, with realization of or failure to realize second level understanding or misunderstanding on the basis of first level agreement or disagreement. Theoretically, there is no end to these levels.

In order to handle such complexity more easily we can use a shorthand. Let A stand for agreement and D for disagreement. Let U stand for understanding and M for misunderstanding. Let R stand for realization of understanding or misunderstanding, and F for failure to realize understanding or misunderstanding. Then R U A U R can mean, when applied to husband and wife, that husband realizes his wife understands they are in agreement, and that she realizes that he understands.

Thus:

Husband	Wife		Husband	Wife
R	U	A	U	R

On the other hand

Husband	Wife		Husband	Wife
F	M	D	M	F

would mean:

That husband and wife disagree; they both misunderstand each other, and both fail to realize their mutual misunderstanding.

There are many ramifications to this scheme that have been gone into in some detail elsewhere.*

* Laing, Phillipson and Lee, op. cit.

The possibilities of the three levels of perspective can be put together as follows.*

	Realization		Failure of Realization	
	under-standing	misunder-standing	under-standing	misunder-standing
agreement	R U A	R M A	F U A	F M A
disagree-ment	R U D	R M D	F U D	F M D

It makes a difference, presumably, to many people whether they think they are in agreement with what most people think (second level): and whether they think that most people regard them as like themselves (third level). It is possible to think what everyone else thinks and to believe that one is in a minority. It is possible to think what few people think and to suppose that one is in the majority. It is possible to feel that They feel one is like Them when one is not, and They do not. It is possible to say: I believe this, but They believe that, so I'm sorry, there is nothing I can do.

Them

Gossip and scandal are always and everywhere elsewhere. Each person is the other to the others. The members of a scandal network may be unified by ideas to which no one will admit in his own person. Each person is thinking of what he thinks the other thinks. The other, in turn, thinks of what yet another thinks. Each person does not mind a

* The sociologist Thomas Scheff has pointed out that, whereas all these cells are empirically possible in two-person relations, two of them may be null cases in group conditions, viz. R M A and R M D.

coloured lodger, but each person's neighbour does. Each person, however, is a neighbour of his neighbour. What They think is held with conviction. It is indubitable and it is incontestable. The scandal group is a series of others which each serial number repudiates in himself.

It is always the others, and always elsewhere, and each person feels unable to make any difference to Them. I have no objection to my daughter marrying a Gentile *really*, but we live in a Jewish neighbourhood after all. Such collective power is in proportion to each person's creation of this power and his own impotence.

This is seen very clearly in the following inverted Romeo and Juliet situation.

John and Mary have a love affair, and just as they are ending it Mary finds she is pregnant. Both families are informed. Mary does not want to marry John. John does not want to marry Mary. But John thinks Mary wants him to marry her, and Mary does not want to hurt John's feelings by telling him that she does not want to marry him – as she thinks he wants to marry her, and that he thinks she wants to marry him.

The two families, however, compound the confusion considerably. Mary's mother takes to bed screaming and in tears because of the disgrace – what people are saying about the way she brought her daughter up. She does not mind the situation 'in itself', especially as the girl is going to be married, but she takes to heart what everyone will be saying. No one in their own person in either family (' . . . if it only affected me . . .') is in the least concerned for their own sake, but everyone is very concerned about the effect of 'gossip' and 'scandal' on everyone else. The concern focuses itself mainly on the boy's father and the girl's mother, both of whom require to be consoled at great length for the terrible blow. The boy's father is worried about what the girl's mother will think of him. The girl's mother is worried about what 'everyone' will think of her. The boy is concerned at what the family thinks he has done to his father, and so on.

The tension spirals up within a few days to the complete engrossment of all members of both families in various forms of tears, wringing of hands, recriminations, apologies.

Typical utterances are:

MOTHER *to* GIRL: Even if he does want to marry you, how can he ever respect you after what people will have been saying about you recently?

GIRL (*some time later*): I had finally got fed up with him just before I found I was pregnant, but I didn't want to hurt his feelings because he was so in love with me.

BOY: If it had not been that I owed it to my father for all he had done for me, I would have arranged that she got rid of it. But then everyone knew by then.

Everyone knew because the son told his father who told his wife who told her eldest son who told his wife ... etc.

Such processes seem to have a dynamism divorced from the individuals. But in this and every other case this process is a form of alienation, intelligible when, and only when, the steps in the vicissitudes of its alienation from each and every person can be retraced back to what at each and every moment is their only origin: the experience and actions of each and every single person.

Now the peculiar thing about Them is that They are created only by each one of us repudiating his own identity. When we have installed Them in our hearts, we are only a plurality of solitudes in which what each person has in common is his allocation to the other of the necessity for his own actions. Each person, however, as

70

other to the other, is the other's necessity. Each denies any internal bond with the others; each person claims his own inessentiality: 'I just carried out my orders. If I had not done so, someone else would have.', 'Why don't you sign? Everyone else has', etc. Yet although I can make no difference, I cannot act differently. No single other person is any more necessary to me than I claim to be to Them. But just as he is 'one of Them' to me, so I am 'one of Them' to him. In this collection of reciprocal indifference, of reciprocal inessentiality and solitude, there appears to exist no freedom. There is conformity to a *presence* that is everywhere *elsewhere*.

Us

The being of any group from the point of view of the group members themselves is very curious. If I think of you and him as together with me, and others again as not with me, I have already formed two rudimentary syntheses, namely, *We* and *Them*. However, this private act of synthesis is not in itself a group. In order that *We* come into being as a group, it is necessary not only that I regard, let us say, you and him and me as *We*, but that you and he also think of us as *We*. I shall call such an act of experiencing a number of persons as a single collectivity, an act of rudimentary group synthesis. In this case *We*, that is each of Us, me, you and him, have performed acts of rudimentary group synthesis. But at present these are simply three private acts of group synthesis. In order that a group really jell, I must realize that you think of yourself as one of Us, as I do, and that he thinks of himself as one of Us, as you and I do. I must ensure furthermore that both you and he realize that I think of myself with you and him, and you and he must ensure likewise

71

that the other two realize that this We is ubiquitous among us, not simply a private illusion on my, your or his part, shared between two of us but not all three.

In a very condensed form I may put the above paragraph as follows.

I 'interiorize' your and his syntheses, you interiorize his and mine, he interiorizes mine and yours: I interiorize your interiorization of mine and his: you interiorize my interiorization of yours and his. Furthermore, he interiorizes my interiorization of his and yours – a logical ingoing spiral of reciprocal perspectives to infinity.

The group, considered first of all from the point of view of the *experience* of its own members, is not a social object out there in space. It is the quite extraordinary being formed by each person's synthesis of the same multiplicity into *We*, and each person's synthesis of the multiplicity of syntheses.

The group looked at from the outside comes into view as a social object, lending by its appearance and by the apparent processes that go on inside it, credence to the organismic illusion.

This is a mirage; as one approaches closer there is no organism anywhere.

A group whose unification is achieved through the reciprocal interiorization by each of each other, in which neither a 'common object' nor organizational or institutional structures etc. have a primary function as a kind of group 'cement', I shall call a *nexus*.

The unity of the nexus is in the interior of each synthesis. Each such act of synthesis is bound by reciprocal interiority with every other synthesis of the same nexus, in so far as it is also the interiority of every other synthesis. The unity of the nexus is the unification made by each person of the plurality of syntheses.

This social structure of the completely achieved nexus is its *unity as ubiquity*. It is an ubiquity of *heres*, whereas the series of others is always elsewhere, always *there*.

The nexus exists only in so far as each person incarnates the nexus. The nexus is everywhere, in each person, and is nowhere else than in each. The nexus is at the opposite pole from Them in that each person acknowledges affiliation to it, regards the other as coessential to him, and assumes that the other regards him as coessential to the other.

> We are all in the same boat in a stormy sea,
> And we owe each other a terrible loyalty.
>   (G. K. CHESTERTON)

In this group of reciprocal loyalty, of brotherhood unto death, each freedom is reciprocally pledged, one to the other.

In the nexal family the unity of the group is achieved through the experience by each of the group, and the danger to each person (since the person is essential to the nexus, and the nexus is essential to the person) is the dissolution or dispersion of 'the family'. This can come about only by one person after another dissolving it in themselves. A united 'family' exists only as long as each person acts in terms of its existence. Each person may then act on the other person to coerce him (by sympathy, blackmail, indebtedness, guilt, gratitude or naked violence) into maintaining his interiorization of the group unchanged.

The nexal family is then the 'entity' that has to be preserved in each person and served by each person, which one lives and dies for, and which in turn offers life for loyalty and death for desertion. Any defection from the nexus (betrayal, treason, heresy, etc.) is deservedly, by nexus ethics, punishable: and the worst punishment devisable by the 'group men' is exile or ex-communication: group death.

The condition of permanence of such a nexus, whose sole existence is each person's experience of it, is the successful re-invention of whatever gives such experience its *raison d'être*. If there is no external danger, then danger and terror have to be invented and maintained. Each person has to act on the others to maintain the nexus *in them*.

Some families live in perpetual anxiety of what, to them, is an external persecuting world. The members of the family live in a family ghetto, as it were. This is one basis for so-called maternal over-protecton. It is not 'over'-protection from the mother's point of view, nor, indeed, often from the point of view of other members of the family.

The 'protection' that such a family offers its members seems to be based on several preconditions: (i) a phantasy of the external world as extraordinarily dangerous; (ii) the generation of terror inside the nexus at this external danger. The 'work' of the nexus is the generation of this terror. This work is *violence*.

The stability of the nexus is the product of terror generated in its members by the work (violence) done by the members of the group on each other. Such family 'homeostasis' is the product of reciprocities mediated under the statutes of violence and terror.

The highest ethic of the nexus is reciprocal concern. Each person is concerned about what the other thinks, feels, does. He may come to regard it as his *right* to expect the others to be concerned about him, and to regard himself as under an obligation to feel concern towards them in turn. I make no move without feeling it as my right that you should be happy or sad, proud or ashamed, of what I do. Every action of mine is always the concern of the other members of the group. And I regard you as callous if you do not concern yourself about my concern for you when you do anything.

A family can act as gangsters, offering each other mutual protection against each other's violence. It is a reciprocal terrorism, with the offer of protection-security against the violence that each threatens the other with, and is threatened by, if anyone steps out of line.

My concern, my concern for your concern, your concern, and your concern for my concern, etc. is an infinite spiral, upon which rests my pride or shame in my father, sister, brother, my mother, my son, my daughter.

The essential characteristic of the nexus is that every action of one person is expected to have reference to and to influence everyone else. The nature of this influence is expected to be reciprocal.

Each person is expected to be controlled, and to control the others, by the reciprocal effect that each has on the other. To be affected by the others' actions or feelings is 'natural'. It is not 'natural' if father is neither proud nor ashamed of son, daughter, mother etc. According to this ethic, action done to please, to make happy, to show one's gratitude to the other is the highest form of action. This reciprocal transpersonal cause-effect is a self-actualizing presumption. In this 'game', it is a foul to use this interdependence to hurt the other, except in the service of the nexus, but the worst crime of all is to refuse to act in terms of this presumption.

Examples of this in action are:

Peter gives Paul something. If Paul is not pleased, or refuses the gift, he is ungrateful for what is being done for him. Or: Peter is made unhappy if Paul does something.

75

Therefore if Paul does it he is making Peter unhappy. If Peter is made unhappy, Paul is inconsiderate, callous, selfish, ungrateful. Or: if Peter is prepared to make sacrifices for Paul, so Paul should be prepared to make sacrifices for Peter, or else he is selfish, ungrateful, callous, ruthless, etc.

'Sacrifice' under these circumstances consists in Peter impoverishing himself to do something for Paul. It is the tactic of *enforced debt*. One way of putting this is that each person *invests in the other*.

The group, whether We, or You or Them, is not a new individual or organism or hyperorganism on the social scene; it has no agency of its own, it has no consciousness of its own. Yet we may shed our own blood and the blood of others for this bloodless presence.

The group is a reality of some kind or other. But what sort of reality? The We is a form of unification of a plurality composed by those who share the common experience of its ubiquitous invention among them.

From outside, a group of Them may come into view in another way. It is still a type of unification imposed on a multiplicity, but this time those who invent the unification expressly do not themselves compose it. Here, I am of course not referring to the outsider's perception of a We already constituted from within itself. The Them comes into view as a sort of social mirage. The Reds, the Whites, the Blacks, the Jews. In the human scene, however, such mirages can be self-actualizing. The invention of Them creates Us, and We may require to invent Them to re-invent Ourselves.

One of the most tentative forms of solidarity between us is when we each want the same thing, but want nothing from each other. We are united, say by a common desire to get the last seat on the train, or to get the best bargain at the Sale. We might gladly cut each other's throat, we may nevertheless feel a certain bond between us, a negative unity, so to say, in that each perceives the other as redundant, and each person's metaperspective shows him that he is redundant for the other. Each as other-for-the-other is one-too-many. In this case, we share a desire to appropriate the same common object or objects: food, land, a social position, real or imagined, but share nothing between ourselves, and do not wish to. Two men both love the same woman, two people both want the same house, two applicants both want the same job. This common object can thus both separate and unite at the same time. A key question is whether it can give itself to all, or not. How *scarce* is it?

The object may be animal, vegetable, mineral, human or divine, real or imaginary, single or plural. A human object uniting people, for instance, is the pop singer in relation to his fans. All can possess him, albeit magically. When this magic confronts the other order of reality, one finds the idol in danger of being torn to shreds by the frenzy of fans seeking any bit of him they can tear off.

The object may be plural. Two rival firms engage in intense competitive advertising, each under the impression that they are losing their consumers to the other. Market research reveals sometimes how riven with phantasy is the scene of such social multiplicities. The laws governing the perception, invention and maintenance of such social beings as 'the consumers' are undiscovered.

The common bond between Us may be the other. The Other may not be even as localized as a definable Them that one can point to. In the social cohesion of scandal, gossip, unavowed racial discrimination, the Other is everywhere and nowhere. The Other that governs everyone is everyone in his position, not of self, but as other. Every self, however, disavows being himself that other that he is for the Other. The Other is everyone's experience. Each person can do nothing because of the other. The other is everywhere elsewhere.

Perhaps the most intimate way We can be united is through each of us being in, and having inside ourselves, the same presence. This is nonsense in any external sense, but here we are exploring a mode of experience which does not recognize the distinctions of analytic logic.

We find this demonic group mysticism repeatedly evoked in the pre-war speeches at Nazi Nuremberg Rallies. Rudolf Hess proclaims: We are the Party, the Party is Germany, Hitler is the Party, Hitler is Germany, and so on.

We are Christians in so far as we are brothers in Christ. We are in Christ and Christ is in each one of us.

No group can be expected to be kept together for long on the pure flame of such unified experience. Groups are liable to disappear through attacks from other groups, or through inability to sustain themselves against the ravages of starvation and disease, from splits through internal dissensions, and so on. But the simplest and perennial threat to all groups comes from the simple defection of its members. This is the danger of evaporation, as it were.

Under the form of group loyalty, brotherhood and love, there is introduced an ethic whose basis is my right to afford the other protection from my violence if he is loyal to me, and to expect his protection from his violence if I am loyal to him, and my obligation to terrorize him with the threat of my violence if he does not remain loyal.

It is the ethic of the Gadarene swine, to remain true, one for all and all for one, as we plunge in brotherhood to our destruction.

Let there be no illusions about the brotherhood of man. My brother, as dear to me as I am to myself, my twin, my double, my flesh and blood, may be a fellow lyncher as well as a fellow martyr, and in either case is liable to meet his death at my hand if he chooses to take a different view of the situation.

The brotherhood of man is evoked by particular men according to their circumstances. But it seldom extends to all men. In the name of our freedom and our brotherhood we are prepared to blow up the other half of mankind, and to be blown up in turn.

The matter is of life or death importance in the most urgent possible sense, since it is on the basis of such primitive social phantasies of who and what are I and you, he and she, We and Them, that the world is linked or separated, that we die, kill, devour, tear and are torn apart, descend to hell or ascend to heaven, in short, that we conduct our lives. What is the 'being' of 'The Reds' to you and me? What is the nature of the presence conjured up by the incantation of this magic sound? Are we sympathizers with 'the East'? Do we feel we have to threaten, deter, placate 'it' or 'her' or 'him'? 'Russia' or 'China' have 'being' nowhere else than in the phantasy of everyone, including the 'Russians' and 'Chinese': nowhere and everywhere. A 'being' phantasied by 'The Russians' as what they are in, which they have to defend, and phantasied by the non-Russians as an alien super-subject-object, from whom one has to defend one's 'freedom', is such that if we all act in terms of such mass serialized preontological phantasy we may all be destroyed by a 'being' that never was, except in so far as we *all* invented her or it or him.

The specifically human feature of human groupings can be exploited to turn them into the semblance of non-human systems.

We do not now suppose that chemical elements combine together *because* they love each other. Atoms do not explode out of hatred. It is men who act out of love and hatred, who combine for defence, attack, or pleasure in each other's company.

All those people who seek to control the behaviour of large numbers of other people work on the *experiences* of those other people. Once people can be induced to experience a situation in a similar way, they can be expected to behave in similar ways. Induce people all to want the same thing, hate the same things, feel the same threat, then their behaviour is already captive – you have acquired your consumers or your cannon-fodder. Induce a common perception of Negroes as subhuman, or the Whites as vicious and effete, and behaviour can be concerted accordingly.

However much experience and action can be transformed into quantitively interchangeable units, the schema for the intelligibility of group structures and permanence is of quite a different order from the schema we employ when we are explaining relative constancies in physical systems. In the latter case, we do not, in the same way, retrace the constancy of a pattern back to the reciprocal interiorization of the pattern by whatever one regards as the units comprising it. The inertia of human groups, however, which appear as the very negation of praxis, is in fact the product of praxis and nothing else. This group inertia can only be an instrument of mystification if it is taken to be part of the 'natural order of things'. The ideological abuse of such an idea is obvious. It so clearly serves the interests of those whose interest it is to have people believe that the *status quo* is of the 'natural order', ordained Divinely or by 'natural' laws. What is less immediately obvious, but no less confusing, is the application of an epistemological schema, derived from natural systems, to human groups. The theoretical stance here only serves to intensify the dissociation of praxis from structure.

The group becomes a machine – and it is forgotten that it is a man-made machine in which the machine is the very men who make it. It is quite unlike a machine made by men, which can have an existence of its own. The group is men themselves arranging themselves in patterns, strata, assuming and assigning different powers, functions, roles, rights, obligations and so on.

The group cannot become an entity separate from men, but men can form circles to encircle other men. The patterns in space and time, their relative permanence and rigidity, do not turn at any time into a natural system or a hyperorganism, although the phantasy can develop, and men can start to live by the phantasy that the relative permanence in space-time of patterns and patterns of patterns are what they must live and die for.

It is as though we all preferred to die to preserve our shadows.

For the group can be nothing else than the multiplicity of the points of view and actions of its members, and this remains true even where, through the interiorization of this multiplicity as synthesized by each, this synthesized multiplicity becomes ubiquitous in space and enduring in time.

It is just as well that man is a social animal, since the

sheer complexity and contradiction of the social field in which he has to live is so formidable. This is so even with the fantastic simplifications that are imposed on this complexity, some of which we have examined above.

Our society is a plural one in many senses. Any one person is likely to be a participant in a number of groups, which may have not only different membership, but quite different forms of unification.

Each group requires more or less radical internal transformation of the persons who comprise it. Consider the metamorphoses that the one man may go through in one day as he moves from one mode of sociality to another – family man, speck of crowd dust, functionary in the organization, friend. These are not simply different roles: each is a whole past and present and future, offering differing options and constraints, different degrees of change or inertia, different kinds of closeness and distance, different sets of rights and obligations, different pledges and promises.

I know of no theory of the individual that fully recognizes this. There is every temptation to start with a notion of some supposed basic personality, but halo effects are not reducible to one internal system. The tired family man at the office and the tired business man at home attest to the fact that people carry over, not just one set of internal objects, but *various internalized social modes of being** from one context to another, often grossly contradictory.

Nor are there such constant emotions or sentiments as love, hate, anger, trust or mistrust. Whatever generalized definitions can be made of each of these at the highest levels of abstraction, specifically and concretely, each

* See 'Individual and Family Structure', in *Psychoanalytic Studies of the Family*, edited by P. Lomasz (London: Hogarth Press, 1966).

emotion is always found in one or another inflection according to the group mode it occurs in. There are no 'basic' emotions, instincts, or personality, outside of the relationships a person has within one or other social context.*

There is a race against time. It is just possible that a further transformation is possible if men can come to experience themselves as 'One of Us'. If, even on the basis of the crassest self interest, we can realize that We and Them must be transcended in the totality of the human race, if we in destroying them are not to destroy us all.

As war continues, both sides come more and more to resemble each other. The uroborus eats its own tail. The wheel turns full circle. Shall we realize that We and Them are shadows of each other? We are Them to Them as They are Them to Us. When will the veil be lifted? When will the charade turn to Carnival? Saints may still be kissing lepers. It is high time that the leper kissed the saint.

* This chapter, in particular, owes a great deal to *Critique de la Raison Dialectique* (1960) by J. P. Sartre. It is summarized in *Reason and Violence* (1964), London: Tavistock Publications, by R. D. Laing and David Cooper.

Chapter 5

The Schizophrenic Experience

JONES (*laughs loudly, then pauses*): I'm McDougal myself. (*This actually is not his name.*)

SMITH: What do you do for a living, little fellow? Work on a ranch or something?

J: No, I'm a civilian seaman. Supposed to be high muckamuck society.

S: A singing recording machine, huh? I guess a recording machine sings sometimes. If they're adjusted right. Mm-hm. I thought that was it. My towel, mm-hm. We'll be going back to sea in about – eight or nine months though. Soon as we get our – destroyed parts repaired. (*Pause*)

J: I've got lovesickness, secret love.

S: Secret love, huh? (*Laughs*)

J: Yeah.

S: I ain't got any secret love.

J: I fell in love, but I don't feed any woo – that sits over – looks something like me – walking around over there.

S: My, oh, my only one, my only love is the shark. Keep out of the way of him.

J: Don't they know I have a life to live? (*Long pause*)

S: Do you work at the air base? Hm?

J: You know what I think of work. I'm thirty-three in June, do you mind?

S: June?

J: Thirty-three years old in June. This stuff goes out the window after I live this, uh – leave this hospital. So I lay off cigarettes, I'm a spatial condition, from outer space myself, no shit.

S (*laughs*): I'm a real space ship from across.

J: A lot of people talk, uh – that way, like crazy, but Believe It or Not by Ripley, take it or leave it – alone it's in the *Examiner*, it's in the comic section, Believe It or Not by Ripley,

Robert E. Ripley, Believe It or Not, but we don't have to believe anything, unless I feel like it. (*Pause*) Every little rosette – too much alone. (*Pause*)

s: Could be possible. (*Phrase inaudible because of aeroplane noise*)

J: I'm a civilian seaman.

s: Could be possible. (*Sighs.*) I take my bath in the ocean.

J: Bathing stinks. You know why? Cause you can't quit when you feel like it. You're in the service.

s: I can quit whenever I feel like quitting. I can get out when I feel like getting out.

J (*talking at the same time*): Take me. I'm a civilian, I can quit.

s: Civilian?

J: Go my – my way.

s: I guess we have, in port, civilian. (*Long pause*)

J: What do they want with us?

s: Hm?

J: What do they want with you and me?

s: What do they want with you and me? How do I know what they want with you? I know what they want with me. I broke the law, so I have to pay for it. (*Silence*)*

This is a conversation between two persons diagnosed as schizophrenic. What does this diagnosis mean?

To regard the gambits of Smith and Jones as due *primarily* to some psychological deficit is rather like supposing that a man doing a handstand on a bicycle on a tightrope 100 feet up with no safety net is suffering from an inability to stand on his own two feet. We may well ask why these people have to be, often brilliantly, so devious, so elusive, so adept at making themselves unremittingly incomprehensible.

In the last decade, a radical shift of outlook has been

* J. Haley, *Strategies of Psychotherapy* (New York: Grune and Stratton, 1963) pages 99–100.

occuring in psychiatry. This has entailed the questioning of old assumptions, based on the attempts of nineteenth-century psychiatrists to bring the frame of clinical medicine to bear on their observations. Thus the subject matter of psychiatry was thought of as mental illness; one thought of mental physiology and mental pathology, one looked for signs and symptoms, made one's diagnosis, assessed prognosis and prescribed treatment. According to one's philosophical bias, one looked for the aetiology of these mental illnesses in the mind, in the body, in the environment, or in inherited propensities.

The term 'schizophrenia' was coined by a Swiss psychiatrist, Bleuler, who worked within this frame of reference. In using the term schizophrenia, I am not referring to any condition that I suppose to be mental rather than physical, or to an illness, like pneumonia, but to a label that some people pin on other people under certain social circumstances. The 'cause' of 'schizophrenia' is to be found by the examination, not of the prospective diagnosee alone, but of the whole social context in which the psychiatric ceremonial is being conducted.*

Once demystified, it is clear, at least, that some people come to behave and to experience themselves and others in ways that are strange and incomprehensible to most people, including themselves. If this behaviour and experience falls into certain broad categories, they are liable to be diagnosed as subject to a condition called schizophrenia. By present calculation almost one in every 100 children born will fall into this category at some time

* See H. Garfinkel, 'Conditions of Successful Degradation Ceremonies', *American Journal of Sociology*, LXI, 1956, pages 420–24; also R. D. Laing, 'Ritualisation in Abnormal Behaviour' in *Ritualisation of Behaviour in Animals and Man* (Royal Society, Philosophical Transactions, Series B (in press)).

or other before the age of forty-five, and in the U.K. at the moment there are roughly 60,000 men and women in mental hospitals, and many more outside hospital, who are termed schizophrenic.

A child born today in the U.K. stands a ten times greater chance of being admitted to a mental hospital than to a university, and about one fifth of mental hospital admissions are diagnosed schizophrenic. This can be taken as an indication that we are driving our children mad more effectively than we are genuinely educating them. Perhaps it is our very way of educating them that is driving them mad.

Most but not all psychiatrists still think that people they call schizophrenic suffer from an inherited predisposition to act in predominantly incomprehensible ways, that some as yet undetermined genetic afctor (possibly a genetic morphism) transacts with a more or less ordinary environment to induce biochemical-endocrinological changes which in turn generate what we observe as the behavioural signs of a subtle underlying organic process.

But it is wrong to impute to someone a hypothetical disease of unknown aetiology and undiscovered pathology unless *he* can prove otherwise.*

The schizophrenic is someone who has queer experiences and/or is acting in a queer way, from the point of view usually of his relatives and of ourselves. . . .

That the diagnosed patient is suffering from a pathological process is either a fact, or an hypothesis, an assumption, or a judgement.

To regard it as fact is unequivocally false. To regard it as an hypothesis is legitimate. It is unnecessary either to make the assumption or to pass judgement.

* See T. Szasz, *The Myth of Mental Illness* (London: Secker & Warburg, 1962).

The psychiatrist, adopting his clinical stance in the presence of the pre-diagnosed person, whom he is already looking at and listening to as a patient, has tended to come to believe that he is in the presence of the 'fact' of schizophrenia. He acts as if its existence were an established fact. He then has to discover its cause or multiple aetiological factors, to assess its prognosis, and to treat its course. The heart of the illness then resides outside the agency of the person. That is, the illness is taken to be a process that the person is subject to or undergoes, whether genetic, constitutional, endogenous, exogenous, organic or psychological, or some mixture of them all.*

Many psychiatrists are now becoming much more cautious about adopting this starting point. But what might take its place?

In understanding the new viewpoint on schizophrenia, we might remind ourselves of the six blind men and the elephant: one touched its body and said it was a wall, another touched an ear and said it was a fan, another a leg and thought it was a pillar, and so on. The problem is sampling, and the error is incautious extrapolation.

The old way of sampling the behaviour of schizophrenics was by the method of clinical examination. The following is an example of the type of examination conducted at the turn of the century. The account is given by the German psychiatrist Emil Kraepelin in his own words.

Gentlemen, the cases that I have to place before you today are peculiar. First of all, you see a servant-girl, aged twenty-four, upon whose features and frame traces of great emaciation can be plainly seen. In spite of this, the patient is in continual movement, going a few steps forward, then back again; she

* R. D. Laing and A. Esterson, *Sanity, Madness and the Family, Volume I: Families of Schizophrenics* (London: Tavistock Publications, 1964; New York: Basic Books, 1965) page 4.

plaits her hair, only to unloose it the next minute. *On attempting to stop her movement*, we meet with unexpectedly strong resistance; *if I place myself in front of her with my arms spread out* in order to stop her, if she cannot push me on one side, she suddenly turns and slips through under my arms, so as to continue her way. *If one takes firm hold* of her, she distorts her usually rigid, expressionless features with deplorable weeping, that only ceases so soon as one lets her have her own way. We notice besides that she holds a crushed piece of bread spasmodically clasped in the fingers of the left hand, which she absolutely *will not allow to be forced from her*. The patient does not trouble in the least about her surroundings so long as you leave her alone. *If you prick her in the forehead with a needle*, she scarcely winces or turns away, and leaves the needle quietly sticking there without letting it disturb her restless, beast-of-prey-like wandering backwards and forwards. *To questions* she answers almost nothing, at the most shaking her head. But from time to time she wails: 'O dear God! O dear God! O dear mother! O dear mother!', always repeating uniformly the same phrases.*

Here are a man and a young girl. If we see the situation purely in terms of Kraepelin's point of view, it all immediately falls into place. He is sane, she is insane: he is rational, she is irrational. This entails looking at the patient's actions out of the context of the situation as she experienced it. But if we take Kraepelin's actions (in italics) – he tries to stop her movements, stands in front of her with arms outspread, tries to force a piece of bread out of her hand, sticks a needle in her forehead, and so on – out of the context of the situation as experienced and defined by him, how extraordinary *they* are!

A feature of the interplay between psychiatrist and patient is that if the patient's part is taken out of con-

* E. Kraepelin, *Lectures on Clinical Psychiatry*, edited by T. Johnstone (London: Baillière, Tindall and Cox, 1906) pages 30–31.

text, as is done in the clinical description, it might seem very odd. The psychiatrist's part, however, is taken as the very touchstone for our common-sense view of normality. The psychiatrist, as *ipso facto* sane, shows that the patient is out of contact with him. The fact that he is out of contact with the patient shows that there is something wrong with the patient, but not with the psychiatrist.

But if one ceases to identify with the clinical posture, and looks at the psychiatrist-patient couple without such presuppositions, then it is difficult to sustain this naïve view of the situation.

Psychiatrists have paid very little attention to the *experience* of the patient. Even in psychoanalysis there is an abiding tendency to suppose that the schizophrenic's experiences are somehow unreal or invalid; one can make sense out of them only by interpreting them; without truth-giving interpretations the patient is enmeshed in a world of delusions and self-deception. Kaplan, an American psychologist, in an introduction to an excellent collection of self-reports on the experience of being psychotic, says very justly:

> With all virtue on his side, he (the psychiatrist or psychoanalyst) reaches through the subterfuges and distortions of the patient and exposes them to the light of reason and insight. In this encounter between the psychiatrist and patient, the efforts of the former are linked with science and medicine, with understanding and care. What the patient experiences is tied to illness and irreality, to perverseness and distortion. The process of psychotherapy consists in large part of the patient's abandoning his false subjective perspectives for the therapist's objective ones. But the essence of this conception is that the psychiatrist understands what is going on, and the patient does not.*

* B. Kaplan (ed.), *The Inner World of Mental Illness* (New York and London: Harper and Row, 1964) page vii.

H. S. Sullivan used to say to young psychiatrists when they came to work with him, 'I want you to remember that in the present state of our society, the patient is right, and you are wrong.' This is an outrageous simplification. I mention it to loosen any fixed ideas that are no less outrageous, that the psychiatrist is right, and the patient wrong. I think however, that schizophrenics have more to teach psychiatrists about the inner world than psychiatrists their patients.

A different picture begins to develop if the interaction between patients themselves is studied without presuppositions. One of the best accounts here is by the American sociologist, Erving Goffman.

Goffman spent a year as an assistant physical therapist in a large mental hospital of some 7,000 beds, near Washington. His lowly staff status enabled him to fraternize with the patients in a way that upper echelons of the staff were unable to do. One of his conclusions is:

There is an old saw that no clearcut line can be drawn between normal people and mental patients: rather there is a continuum with the well-adjusted citizen at one end and the full-fledged psychotic at the other. I must argue that after a period of acclimatization in a mental hospital the notion of a continuum seems very presumptuous. A community is a community. Just as it is bizarre to those not in it, so it is natural, even if unwanted, to those who live it from within. The system of dealings that patients have with one another does not fall at one end of anything, but rather provides one example of human association, to be avoided, no doubt, but also to be filed by the student in a circular cabinet along with all the other examples of association that he can collect.*

* E. Goffman, *Asylums. Essays on the Social Situation of Mental Patients and Other Inmates* (New York: Doubleday-Anchor Books, 1961) page 303.

A large part of his study is devoted to a detailed documentation of how it comes about that a person, in being put in the role of patient, tends to become defined as a non-agent, as a non-responsible object, to be treated accordingly, and even comes to regard himself in this light.

Goffman shows also that by shifting one's focus from seeing the person out of context, to seeing him in his context, behaviour that might seem quite unintelligible, at best to be explained as some intra-psychic regression or organic deterioration, can make quite ordinary human sense. He does not just describe such behaviour 'in' mental hospital patients, he describes it within the context of personal interaction and the system in which it takes place.

... there is a vicious circle process at work. Persons who are lodged on 'bad' wards find that very little equipment of any kind is given them – clothes may be taken away from them each night, recreational materials may be withheld, and only heavy wooden chairs and benches provided for furniture. Acts of hostility against the institution have to rely on limited, ill-designed devices, such as banging a chair against the floor or striking a sheet of newspaper sharply so as to make an annoying explosive sound. And the more inadequate this equipment is to convey rejection of the hospital, the more the act appears as a psychotic symptom, and the more likely it is that management feels justified in assigning the patient to a bad ward. When a patient finds himself in seclusion, naked and without visible means of expression, he may have to rely on tearing up his mattress, if he can, or writing with faeces on the wall – actions management takes to be in keeping with the kind of person who warrants seclusion.*

It is on account of their behaviour outside hospital,

* E. Goffman: op. cit., page 306.

however, that people get diagnosed as schizophrenic and admitted to hospital in the first place.

There have been many studies of social factors in relation to schizophrenia. These include attempts to discover whether schizophrenia occurs more or less frequently in one or other ethnic group, social class, sex, ordinal position in the family, and so on. The conclusion from such studies has often been that social factors do not play a significant role in the 'aetiology of schizophrenia'. This begs the question, and moreover such studies do not get close enough to the relevant situation. If the police wish to determine whether a man has died of natural causes or has committed suicide, or been murdered, they do not look up prevalence or incidence figures. They investigate the circumstances attendant upon each single case in turn. Each investigation is an original research project, and it comes to an end when enough evidence has been gathered to answer the relevant questions.

It is only in the last ten years that the immediate interpersonal environment of 'schizophrenics' has come to be studied in its interstices. This work was prompted, in the first place, by psychotherapists who formed the impression that, if their patients were *disturbed*, their families were often very *disturbing*. Psychotherapists, however, remained committed by their technique not to study the families directly. At first the focus was mainly on the mothers (who are always the first to get the blame for everything), and a 'schizophrenogenic' mother was postulated, who was supposed to generate disturbance in her child.

Next, attention was paid to the husbands of these undoubtedly unhappy women, then to the parental and parent-child interactions (rather than to each person in the family separately), then to the nuclear family group of parents and children, and finally to the whole relevant network of people in and around the family, including the grandparents of patients. By the time our own researches started, this methodological breakthrough had been made and, in addition, a major theoretical advance had been achieved.

This was the 'double-bind' hypothesis, whose chief architect was the anthropologist Gregory Bateson. This theory*, first published in 1956, represented a theoretical advance of the first order. The germ of the idea developed in Bateson's mind in studying New Guinea in the 1930s. In New Guinea the culture had, as all cultures have, built-in techniques for maintaining its own inner balance. One technique, for example, that served to neutralize dangerous rivalry, was sexual transvestism. However, missionaries and the occidental government tended to object to such practices. The culture was therefore caught between the risk of external extermination or internal disruption.

Together with research workers in California, Bateson brought this paradigm of an insoluble 'can't win' situation, specifically destructive of self-identity, to bear on the internal family pattern of communication of diagnosed schizophrenics.

The studies of the families of schizophrenics conducted at Palo Alto, California, Yale University, the Pennsylvania Psychiatric Institute, and at the National Institute of Mental Health, among other places, have all shown that the person who gets diagnosed is part of a wider network of extremely disturbed and disturbing patterns of communication. In all these places, to the best of my knowledge, *no* schizophrenic has been studied

* G. Bateson, D. D. Jackson, J. Haley, J. and J. Weakland, 'Towards a theory of schizophrenia', *Behavioural Science*, Volume I, number 251, 1956.

whose disturbed pattern of communication has not been shown to be a reflection of, and reaction to, the disturbed and disturbing pattern characterizing his or her family of origin. This is matched in our own researches.*

In over 100 cases where we† have studied the actual circumstances around the social event when one person comes to be regarded as schizophrenic, it seems to us that *without exception* the experience and behaviour that gets labelled schizophrenic is *a special strategy that a person invents in order to live in an unlivable situation*. In his life situation the person has come to feel he is in an untenable position. He cannot make a move, or make no move, without being beset by contradictory and paradoxical pressures and demands, pushes and pulls, both internally, from himself, and externally, from those around him. He is, as it were, in a position of checkmate.

This state of affairs may not be perceived as such by any of the people in it. The man at the bottom of the heap may be being crushed and suffocated to death without anyone noticing, much less intending it. The situation here described is impossible to see by studying the different people in it singly. The social system, not single individuals extrapolated from it, must be the object of study.

We know that the biochemistry of the person is highly sensitive to social circumstance. That a checkmate situation occasions a biochemical response which, in turn, facilitates or inhibits certain types of experience and behaviour is plausible *a priori*.

The behaviour of the diagnosed patient is part of a

* R. D. Laing and A. Esterson, *Sanity, Madness and the Family* (London: Tavistock Publications, 1964; New York: Basic Books, 1965).

† Drs David Cooper, A. Esterson and myself.

much larger network of disturbed behaviour. The contradictions and confusions 'internalized' by the individual must be looked at in their larger social contexts.

Something is wrong somewhere, but it can no longer be seen exclusively or even primarily 'in' the diagnosed patient.

Nor is it a matter of laying the blame at anyone's door. The untenable position, the 'can't win' double-bind, the situation of checkmate, is by definition *not obvious* to the protagonists. Very seldom is it a question of contrived, deliberate, cynical lies or a ruthless intention to drive someone crazy, although this occurs more commonly than is usually supposed. We have had parents tell us that they would rather their child was mad than that he or she realize the truth. Though even here, it is because they say that 'it is a mercy' that the person is 'out of his mind'. A checkmate position cannot be described in a few words. The whole situation has to be grasped before it can be seen that no move is possible, and making no move is equally unlivable.

With these reservations, the following is an example of an interaction given in *The Self and Others** between a father, mother, and son of twenty recovering from a schizophrenic episode.

In this session the patient was maintaining that he was selfish, while his parents were telling him that he was not. The psychiatrist asked the patient to give an example of what he meant by 'selfish'.

SON: Well, when my mother sometimes makes me a big meal and I won't eat it if I don't feel like it.
FATHER: But he wasn't always like that, you know. He's always been a good boy.

* R. D. Laing (London: Tavistock Publications, 1961; Chicago: Quadrangle Press, 1962).

MOTHER: That's his illness, isn't it, doctor? He was never ungrateful. He was always most polite and well brought up. We've done our best by him.

SON: No, I've always been selfish and ungrateful. I've no self-respect.

FATHER: But you have.

SON: I could have, if you respected me. No one respects me. Everyone laughs at me. I'm the joke of the world. I'm the joker all right.

FATHER: But, son, I respect you, because I respect a man who respects himself.

It is hardly surprising that the person in his terror may stand in curious postures in an attempt to control the irresolvably contradictory social 'forces' that are controlling him, that he projects the inner on to the outer, introjects the outer on to the inner, that he tries in short to protect himself from destruction by every means that he has, by projection, introjection, splitting, denial and so on.

Gregory Bateson, in a brilliant introduction to a nineteenth-century autobiographical account of schizophrenia, has said this:

It would appear that once precipitated into psychosis the patient has a course to run. He is, as it were, embarked upon a voyage of discovery which is only completed by his return to the normal world, to which he comes back with insights different from those of the inhabitants who never embarked on such a voyage. Once begun, a schizophrenic episode would appear to have as definite a course as an initiation ceremony – a death and rebirth – into which the novice may have been precipitated by his family life or by adventitious circumstances, but which in its course is largely steered by endogenous process.

In terms of this picture, spontaneous remission is no problem. This is only the final and natural outcome of the total process. What needs to be explained is the failure of many who embark upon this voyage to return from it. *Do these encounter* *circumstances either in family life or in institutional care so grossly maladaptive that even the richest and best organized hallucinatory experience cannot save them?**

I am in substantial agreement with this view.

A revolution is currently going on in relation to sanity and madness, both inside and outside psychiatry. The clinical point of view is giving way before a point of view that is both existential and social.

From an ideal vantage point on the ground, a formation of planes may be observed in the air. One plane may be out of formation. But the whole formation may be off course. The plane that is 'out of formation' may be abnormal, bad or 'mad' from the point of view of the formation. But the formation itself may be bad or mad from the point of view of the ideal observer. The plane that is out of formation may be also more or less off course than the formation itself is.

The 'out of formation' criterion is the clinical positivist criterion.

The 'off course' criterion is the ontological. One requires to make two judgements along these different parameters. In particular, it is of fundamental importance not to confuse the person who may be 'out of formation' by telling him he is 'off course' if he is not. It is of fundamental importance not to make the positivist mistake of assuming that, because a group are 'in formation', this means they are necessarily 'on course'. This is the Gadarene swine fallacy. Nor is it necessarily the case that the person who is 'out of formation' is more 'on course' than the formation. There is no need to idealize someone just because he is labelled 'out of formation'. There is also no

* G. Bateson (ed.), *Perceval's Narrative. A Patient's Account of his Psychosis* (Stanford, California: Stanford University Press, 1961) pages xiii–xiv; italics mine.

need to persuade the person who is 'out of formation' that cure consists in getting back into formation. The person who is 'out of formation' is often full of hatred of the formation and fears about being the odd man out.

If the formation is itself off course, then the man who is really to get 'on course' must leave the formation. But it is possible to do so, if one desires, without screeches and screams, and without terrorizing the already terrified formation that one has to leave.

In the diagnostic category of schizophrenic are many different types of sheep and goats.

'Schizophrenia' is a diagnosis, a label applied by some people to others. This does not prove that the labelled person is subject to an essentially pathological process, of unknown nature and origin, going on *in* his or her body. It does not mean that the process is, primarily or secondarily, a *psycho*-pathological one, going on *in* the *psyche* of the person. But it does establish as a social fact that the person labelled is one of Them. It is easy to forget that the process is a hypothesis, to assume that it is a fact, then to pass the judgement that it is biologically maladaptive and, as such, pathological. But social adaptation to a dysfunctional society may be very dangerous. The perfectly adjusted bomber pilot may be a greater threat to species survival than the hospitalized schizophrenic deluded that the Bomb is inside him. Our society may itself have become biologically dysfunctional, and some forms of schizophrenic alienation from the alienation of society may have a sociobiological function that we have not recognized. This holds even if a genetic factor predisposes to some kinds of schizophrenic behaviour. Recent critiques of the work on genetics* and the most

* See for instance: Pekka Tienari, *Psychiatric Illnesses in Identical Twins* (Copenhagen: Munksgaard, 1963).

recent empirical genetic studies, leave this matter open.

Jung suggested some years ago that it would be an interesting experiment to study whether the syndrome of psychiatry runs in families. A pathological process called 'psychiatrosis' may well be found, by the same methods, to be a delineable entity, with somatic correlates and psychic mechanisms, with an inherited or at least constitutional basis, a natural history, and a doubtful prognosis.

The most profound recent development in psychiatry has been to redefine the basic categories and assumptions of psychiatry itself. We are now in a transitional stage, where we still to some extent continue to use old bottles for new wine. We have to decide whether to use old terms in a new way, or abandon them to the dustbin of history.

There is no such 'condition' as 'schizophrenia', but the label is a social fact and the social fact a *political event*.* This political event, occurring in the civic order of society, imposes definitions and consequences on the labelled person. It is a social prescription that rationalizes a set of social actions whereby the labelled person is annexed by others, who are legally sanctioned, medically empowered, and morally obliged, to become responsible for the person labelled. The person labelled is inaugurated not only into a role, but into a career of patient, by the concerted action of a coalition (a 'conspiracy') of family, G.P., mental health officer, psychiatrists, nurses, psychiatric social workers, and often fellow patients. The 'committed' person labelled as patient, and specifically as 'schizo-phrenic', is degraded from full existential and legal status

* T. Scheff, 'Social Conditions for Rationality: How Urban and Rural Courts Deal with the Mentally Ill,' *Amer. Behav. Scient.*, March, 1964. Also, T. Scheff, 'The Societal Reaction to Deviants: Ascriptive Elements in the Psychiatric Screening of Mental Patients in a Mid-Western State', *Social Problems*, No. 4, Spring, 1964.

as human agent and responsible person, no longer in possession of his own definition of himself, unable to retain his own possessions, precluded from the exercise of his discretion as to whom he meets, what he does. His time is no longer his own and the space he occupies is no longer of his choosing. After being subjected to a degradation ceremonial* known as psychiatric examination he is bereft of his civil liberties in being imprisoned in a total institution† known as a 'mental' hospital. More completely, more radically than anywhere else in our society, he is invalidated as a human being. In the mental hospital he must remain, until the label is rescinded or qualified by such terms as 'remitted' or 'readjusted'. Once a 'schizophrenic' there is a tendency to be regarded as always a 'schizophrenic'.

Now why and how does this happen? And what functions does this procedure serve for the maintenance of the civic order? These questions are only just beginning to be asked, much less answered. Questions and answers have so far been focused on the family as a social subsystem. Socially, this work must now move to further understanding, not only of the internal disturbed and disturbing patterns of communication within families, of the double-binding procedures, the pseudo-mutuality, of what I have called the mystifications and the untenable positions, but also to the meaning of all this within the larger context of the civic order of society – that is, of the *political* order, of the ways persons exercise control and power over one another.

* H. Garfinkel, 'Conditions of Successful Degradation Ceremonies', *American Journal of Sociology*, LXI, 1956.

† E. Goffman, *Asylums. Essays on the Social Situation of Mental Patients and Other Inmates* (New York: Doubleday-Anchor Books, 1961).

Some people labelled schizophrenic (not all, and not necessarily) manifest behaviour in words, gestures, actions (linguistically, paralinguistically and kinetically) that is unusual. Sometimes (not always and not necessarily) this unusual behaviour (manifested to us, the others, as I have said, by sight and sound) expresses, wittingly or unwittingly, unusual experiences that the person is undergoing. Sometimes (not always and not necessarily) these unusual experiences that are expressed by unusual behaviour appear to be part of a potentially orderly, natural sequence of experiences.

This sequence is very seldom allowed to occur because we are so busy 'treating' the patient, whether by chemotherapy, shock therapy, *milieu* therapy, group therapy, psychotherapy, family therapy – sometimes now, in the very best, most advanced places, by the lot.

What we see sometimes in *some* people whom we label and 'treat' as schizophrenics are the behavioural expressions of an experiential drama. But we see this drama in a distorted form that our therapeutic efforts tend to distort further. The outcome of this unfortunate dialectic is a *forme frustre* of a potentially *natural* process, that we do not allow to happen.

In characterizing this sequence in general terms, I shall write *entirely* about a sequence of experience. I shall therefore have to use the language of experience. So many people feel they have to translate 'subjective' events into 'objective' terms in order to be scientific. To be genuinely scientific means having valid knowledge of a chosen domain of reality. So in the following I shall use the language of experience to describe the events of experience. Also, I shall not so much be describing a series of different discrete events but describing a unitary sequence, from different points of view, and using a variety of idioms to do so. I suggest that this natural process, which our labelling and well-intentioned therapeutic efforts distorts and arrests, is as follows.

We start again from the split of our experience into what seems to be two worlds, inner and outer.

The normal state of affairs is that we know little of either and are alienated from both, but that we know perhaps a little more of the outer than the inner. However, the very fact that it is necessary to speak of outer and inner at all implies that an historically-conditioned split has occurred, so that the inner is already as bereft of substance as the outer is bereft of meaning.

We need not be unaware of the 'inner' world. We do not realize its existence most of the time. But many people enter it – unfortunately without guides, confusing outer with inner realities, and inner with outer – and generally lose their capacity to function competently in ordinary relations.

This need not be so. The process of entering into *the other* world from this world, and returning to *this* world from the other world, is as natural as death and giving birth or being born. But in our present world, that is both so terrified and so unconscious of the other world, it is not surprising that when 'reality', the fabric of this world, bursts, and a person enters the other world, he is completely lost and terrified, and meets only incomprehension in others.

Some people wittingly, some people unwittingly, enter or are thrown into more or less total inner space and time. We are socially conditioned to regard total immersion in outer space and time as normal and healthy. Immersion in inner space and time tends to be regarded as anti-social withdrawal, a deviancy, invalid, pathological *per se*, in some sense discreditable.

Sometimes, having gone through the looking glass, through the eye of the needle, the territory is recognized as one's lost home, but most people now in inner space and time are, to begin with, in unfamiliar territory and are frightened and confused. They are lost. They have forgotten that they have been there before. They clutch at chimeras. They try to retain their bearings by compounding their confusion, by projection (putting the inner on to the outer), and introjection (importing outer categories into the inner). They do not know what is happening, and no one is likely to enlighten them.

We defend ourselves violently even from the full range of our egoically limited experience. How much more are we likely to react with terror, confusion and 'defences' against ego-loss experience. There is nothing intrinsically pathological in the experience of ego-loss, but it may be very difficult to find a living context for the journey one may be embarked upon.

The person who has entered this inner realm (if only he is allowed to experience this) will find himself going, or being conducted – one cannot clearly distinguish active from passive here – on a journey.

This journey is experienced as going further 'in', as going back through one's personal life, in and back and through and beyond into the experience of all mankind, of the primal man, of Adam and perhaps even further into the being of animals, vegetables and minerals.

In this journey there are many occasions to lose one's way, for confusion, partial failure, even final shipwreck: many terrors, spirits, demons to be encountered, that may or may not be overcome.

We do not regard it as pathologically deviant to explore a jungle, or to climb Mount Everest. We feel that Columbus was entitled to be mistaken in his construction of what he discovered when he came to the New World. We are far more out of touch with even the nearest approaches of the infinite reaches of inner space than we now are with the reaches of outer space. We respect the voyager, the explorer, the climber, the space man. It makes far more sense to me as a valid project – indeed, as a desperately urgently required project for our time, to explore the inner space and time of consciousness. Perhaps this is one of the few things that still make sense in our historical context. We are so out of touch with this realm that many people can now argue seriously that it does not exist. It is very small wonder that it is perilous indeed to explore such a lost realm. The situation I am suggesting is precisely as though we all had almost total lack of any knowledge whatever of what we call the outer world. What would happen if some of us then started to see, hear, touch, smell, taste things? We would hardly be more confused than the person who first has vague intimations of, and then moves into, inner space and time. This is where the person sitting in a chair labelled catatonic has often gone. He is not at all here: he is all there. He is frequently very mistaken about what he is experiencing, and he probably does not want to experience it. He may indeed be lost. There are very few of us who know the territory in which he is lost, who know how to reach him, and how to find the way back.

No age in the history of humanity has perhaps so lost touch with this natural *healing* process, that implicates *some* of the people whom we label schizophrenic. No age has so devalued it, no age has imposed such prohibitions and deterrences against it, as our own. Instead of the mental hospital, a sort of re-servicing factory for human breakdowns, we need a place where people who have travelled further and, consequently, may be more lost than psychiatrists and other sane people, can find their way *further* into inner space and time, and back again. Instead of the *degradation* ceremonial of psychiatric examination, diagnosis and prognostication, we need, for those who are ready for it (in psychiatric terminology often those who are about to go into a schizophrenic breakdown), an *initiation* ceremonial, through which the person will be guided with full social encouragement and sanction into inner space and time, by people who have been there and back again. Psychiatrically, this would appear as ex-patients helping future patients to go mad.

What is entailed then is:

   (i) a voyage from outer to inner,

   (ii) from life to a kind of death,

   (iii) from going forward to a going back,

   (iv) from temporal movement to temporal standstill,

   (v) from mundane time to aeonic time,

   (vi) from the ego to the self,

   (vii) from being outside (post-birth) back into the womb of all things (pre-birth),

and then subsequently a return voyage from

   (1) inner to outer,

   (2) from death to life,

   (3) from the movement back to a movement once more forward,

   (4) from immortality back to mortality,

   (5) from eternity back to time,

   (6) from self to a new ego,

   (7) from a cosmic foetalization to an existential rebirth.

I shall leave it to those who wish to translate the above elements of this perfectly natural and necessary process into the jargon of psychopathology and clinical psychiatry. This process may be one that all of us need, in one form or another. This process could have a central function in a truly sane society.

I have listed very briefly little more than the headings for an extended study and understanding of a natural sequence of experiential stepping stones that, in some instances, is submerged, concealed, distorted and arrested by the label 'schizophrenia' with its connotations of pathology and consequences of an illness-to-be-cured.

Perhaps we will learn to accord to so-called schizophrenics who have come back to us, perhaps after years, no less respect than the often no less lost explorers of the Renaissance. If the human race survives, future men will, I suspect, look back on our enlightened epoch as a veritable age of Darkness. They will presumably be able to savour the irony of this situation with more amusement than we can extract from it. The laugh's on us. They will see that what we call 'schizophrenia' was one of the forms in which, often through quite ordinary people, the light began to break through the cracks in our all-too-closed minds.

Schizophrenia used to be a new name for dementia praecox – a slow, insidious illness that was supposed to overtake young people in particular, and to be liable to go on to a terminal dementia.

Perhaps we can still retain the now old name, and read into it its etymological meaning: *Schiz* – 'broken'; *Phrenos* – 'soul or heart'.

The schizophrenic in this sense is one who is broken-hearted, and even broken hearts have been known to mend, if we have the heart to let them.

But 'schizophrenia', in this existential sense, has little to do with the clinical examination, diagnosis, prognosis and prescriptions for therapy of 'schizophrenia'.

Chapter 6

Transcendental Experience

WE are living in an age in which the ground is shifting and the foundations are shaking. I cannot answer for other times and places. Perhaps it has always been so. We know it is true today.

In these circumstances, we have all reason to be insecure. When the ultimate basis of our world is in question, we run to different holes in the ground, we scurry into roles, statuses, identities, interpersonal relations. We attempt to live in castles that can only be in the air, because there is no firm ground in the social cosmos on which to build. We are all witnesses to this state of affairs. Each sometimes sees the same fragment of the whole situation differently; often our concern is with different presentations of the original catastrophe.

In this chapter I wish to relate the transcendental experiences that *sometimes* break through in psychosis, to those experiences of the divine that are the living fount of all religion.

In the last chapter I outlined the way in which some psychiatrists are beginning to dissolve their clinical-medical categories of understanding madness. If we can begin to understand sanity and madness in existential social terms, we shall be more able to see clearly the extent to which we all confront common problems and share common dilemmas.

Experience may be judged to be invalidly mad or to be validly mystical. The distinction is not easy. In either case, from a social point of view, such judgements characterize different forms of behaviour, regarded in our society as deviant. People behave in such ways because their experience of themselves is different. It is on the existential meaning of such unusual experience that I wish to focus.

Psychotic experience goes beyond the horizons of our common, that is, our communal sense.

What regions of experience does this lead to? It entails a loss of the usual foundations of the 'sense' of the world that we share with one another. Old purposes no longer seem viable: old meanings are senseless: the distinctions between imagination, dream, external perceptions often seem no longer to apply in the old way. External events may seem magically conjured up. Dreams may seem direct communications from others: imagination may seem to be objective reality.

But most radically of all the very ontological foundations are shaken. The being of phenomena shifts and the phenomena of being may no longer present itself to us as before. There are no supports, nothing to cling to, except perhaps some fragments from the wreck, a few memories, names, sounds, one or two objects, that retain a link with a world long lost. This void may not be empty. It may be peopled by visions and voices, ghosts, strange shapes and apparitions. No one who has not experienced how insubstantial the pageant of external reality can be, how it may fade, can fully realize the sublime and grotesque presences that can replace it, or that can exist alongside it.

When a person goes mad, a profound transposition of his position in relation to all domains of being occurs. His centre of experience moves from ego to Self. Mundane time becomes merely anecdotal, only the eternal matters. The madman is however confused. He muddles ego with self, inner with outer, natural and supernatural. Nevertheless, he often can be to us, even through his profound wretchedness and disintegration, the hierophant of the sacred. An exile from the scene of being as we know it, he is an alien, a stranger, signalling to us from the void in which he is foundering, a void which may be peopled by presences that we do not even dream of. They used to be called demons and spirits, and they used to be known and named. He has lost his sense of self, his feelings, his place in the world as we know it. He tells us he is dead. But we are distracted from our cosy security by this mad ghost that haunts us with his visions and voices that seem so senseless and of which we feel impelled to rid him, cleanse him, cure him.

Madness need not be all breakdown. It may also be break-through. It is potentially liberation and renewal as well as enslavement and existential death.

There are now a growing number of accounts by people who have been through the experience of madness.*

The following is part of one of the earlier contemporary accounts, as recorded by Karl Jaspers in his *General Psychopathology*.†

I believe I caused the illness myself. In my attempt to penetrate the other world I met its natural guardians, the embodiment of my own weaknesses and faults. I first thought these demons were lowly inhabitants of the other world who could play me like a ball because I went into these regions unprepared and lost my way. Later I thought they were split-off parts of my own mind (passions) which existed near me in free space and thrived on my feelings. I believed everyone else had these too but did not perceive them, thanks to the protective and successful deceit of the feeling of personal existence. I thought the latter was an artefact of memory, thought-

* See, for example, the anthology: *The Inner World of Mental Illness* (ed. Kaplan) (New York and London: Harper and Row, 1964), and *Beyond All Reason* by Morag Coate (London: Constable and Co., 1964; Philadelphia: Lippincott, 1965).

† Manchester: Manchester University Press, 1962, pages 417–18.

complexes, etc., a doll that was nice enough to look at from outside but nothing real inside it.

In my case the personal self had grown porous because of my dimmed consciousness. Through it I wanted to bring myself closer to the higher sources of life. I should have prepared myself for this over a long period by invoking in me a higher, impersonal self, since 'nectar' is not for mortal lips. It acted destructively on the animal-human self, split it up into its parts. These gradually disintegrated, the doll was really broken and the body damaged. I had forced untimely access to the 'source of life', the curse of the 'gods' descended on me. I recognized too late that murky elements had taken a hand. I got to know them after they had already too much power. There was no way back. I now had the world of spirits I had wanted to see. The demons came up from the abyss, as guardian Cerberi, denying admission to the unauthorized. I decided to take up the life-and-death struggle. This meant for me in the end a decision to die, since I had to put aside everything that maintained the enemy, but this was also everything that maintained life. I wanted to enter death without going mad and stood before the Sphinx: either thou into the abyss or I!

Then came illumination. I fasted and so penetrated into the true nature of my seducers. They were pimps and deceivers of my dear personal self which seemed as much a thing of naught as they. A larger and more comprehensive self emerged and I could abandon the previous personality with its entire entourage. I saw this earlier personality could never enter transcendental realms. I felt as a result a terrible pain, like an annihilating blow, but I was rescued, the demons shrivelled, vanished and perished. A new life began for me and from now on I felt different from other people. A self that consisted of conventional lies, shams, self-deceptions, memory-images, a self just like that of other people, grew in me again but behind and above it stood a greater and more comprehensive self which impressed me with something of what is eternal, unchanging, immortal and inviolable and which ever since that time has been my protector and refuge. I believe it would be good for many if they were acquainted with such a higher self and that there are people who have attained this goal in fact by kinder means.

Jaspers comments:

Such self-interpretations are obviously made under the influence of delusion-like tendencies and deep psychic forces. They originate from profound experiences and the wealth of such schizophrenic experience calls on the observer as well as on the reflective patient not to take all this merely as a chaotic jumble of contents. Mind and spirit are present in the morbid psychic life as well as in the healthy. But interpretations of this sort must be divested of any causal importance. All they can do is to throw light on content and bring it into some sort of context.

This patient has described with a lucidity I could not improve upon, a very ancient quest, with its pitfalls and dangers. Jaspers still speaks of this experience as morbid, and tends to discount the patient's own construction. Yet both the experience and construction may be valid in their own terms.

Certain *transcendental experiences* seem to me to be the original well-spring of all religions. Some pyschotic people have transcendental experiences. Often (to the best of their recollection), they have never had such experiences before, and frequently they will never have them again. I am not saying, however, that psychotic experience necessarily contains this element more manifestly than sane experience.

We experience in different modes. We perceive external realities, we dream, imagine, have semi-conscious reveries. Some people have visions, hallucinations, experience faces transfigured, see auras, and so on. Most people most of the time experience themselves and others

112

in one or other way that I shall call *egoic*. That is, centrally or peripherally, they experience the world and themselves in terms of a consistent identity, a me-here over against a you-there, within a framework of certain ground structures of space and time, shared with other members of their society.

This identity-anchored, space-and-time-bound experience has been studied philosophically by Kant, and later by the phenomenologists, e.g. Husserl, Merleau-Ponty. Its historical and ontological relativity should be fully realized by any contemporary student of the human scene. Its cultural, socio-economic relativity has become a commonplace among anthropologists and a platitude to the Marxists and neo-Marxists. And yet, with the consensual and interpersonal confirmation it offers, it gives us a sense of ontological security, whose validity we *experience* as self-validating, although metaphysically-historically - ontologically - socio-economically - culturally we know its apparent absolute validity as an illusion.

In fact all religious and all existential philosophies have agreed that such *egoic experience* is a preliminary illusion, a veil, a film of *maya* – a dream to Heraclitus, and to Lao-Tzu, the fundamental illusion of all Buddhism, a state of sleep, of death, of socially accepted madness, a womb state to which one has to die, from which one has to be born.

The person going through ego-loss or transcendental experiences may or may not become in different ways confused. Then he might legitimately be regarded as mad. But to be mad is not necessarily to be ill, notwithstanding that in our culture the two categories have become confused. It is assumed that if a person is mad (whatever that means) then *ipso facto* he is ill (whatever that means). The experience that a person may be absorbed in while to others he appears simply ill-mad, may be for him veritable manna from heaven. The person's whole life may be changed, but it is difficult not to doubt the validity of such vision. Also, not everyone comes back to us again.

Are these experiences simply the effulgence of a pathological process, or of a particular alienation? I do not think they are.

In certain cases, a man blind from birth may have an operation performed which gives him his sight. The result – frequently misery, confusion, disorientation. The light that illumines the madman is an unearthly light. It is not always a distorted refraction of his mundane life situation. He may be irradiated by light from other worlds. It may burn him out.

This 'other' world is not essentially a battlefield wherein psychological forces, derived or diverted, displaced or sublimated from their original object-cathexes are engaged in an illusionary fight – although such forces may obscure these realities, just as they may obscure so-called external realities. When Ivan, in *The Brothers Karamazov* says, 'If God does not exist, everything is permissible', he is *not* saying: 'If my super-ego, in projected form, can be abolished, I can do anything with a good conscience.' He *is* saying: 'If there is *only* my conscience, then there is no ultimate validity for my will.'

Among physicians and priests there should be some who are guides, who can educt the person from this world and induct him to the other. To guide him in it: and to lead him back again.

One enters the other world by breaking a shell: or through a door: through a partition: the curtains part or rise: a veil is lifted. Seven veils: seven seals, seven heavens.

The 'ego' is the instrument for living in *this* world. If

the 'ego' is broken up, or destroyed (by the insurmountable contradictions of certain life situations, by toxins, chemical changes, etc.), then the person may be exposed to other worlds, 'real' in different ways from the more familiar territory of dreams, imagination, perception or phantasy.

The world that one enters, one's capacity to experience it, seems to be partly conditional on the state of one's 'ego'.

Our time has been distinguished, more than by anything else, by a drive to control the external world, and by an almost total forgetfulness of the internal world. If one estimates human evolution from the point of view of knowledge of the external world, then we are in many respects progressing.

If our estimate is from the point of view of the internal world, and of oneness of internal and external, then the judgement must be very different.

Phenomenologically the terms 'internal' and 'external' have little validity. But in this whole realm one is reduced to mere verbal expedients – words are simply the finger pointing to the moon. One of the difficulties of talking in the present day of these matters is that the very existence of inner realities is now called in question.

By 'inner' I mean our way of seeing the external world and all those realities that have no 'external', 'objective' presence – imagination, dreams, phantasies, trances, the realities of contemplative and meditative states, realities that modern man, for the most part, has not the slightest direct awareness of.

For example, nowhere in the Bible is there any argument about the *existence* of gods, demons, angels. People did not first 'believe in' God: they experienced his Presence, as was true of other spiritual agencies. The question was not whether God existed, but whether this particular God was the greatest god of all, or the only God; and what was the relation of the various spiritual agencies to each other. Today, there is a public debate, not as to the trustworthiness of God, the particular place in the spiritual hierarchy of different spirits, etc., but whether God or such spirits *even exist*, or ever have existed.

Sanity today appears to rest very largely on a capacity to adapt to the external world – the interpersonal world, and the realm of human collectivities.

As this external human world is almost completely and totally estranged from the inner, any personal direct awareness of the inner world has already grave risks.

But since society, without knowing it, is *starving* for the inner, the demands on people to evoke its presence in a 'safe' way, in a way that need not be taken seriously, etc., is tremendous – while the ambivalence is equally intense. Small wonder that the list of artists, in say the last 150 years, who have become shipwrecked on these reefs is so long – Hölderlin, John Clare, Rimbaud, Van Gogh, Nietzsche, Antonin Artaud. . . .

Those who survived have had exceptional qualities – a capacity for secrecy, slyness, cunning – a thoroughly realistic appraisal of the risks they run, not only from the spiritual realms that they frequent, but from the hatred of their fellows for anyone engaged in this pursuit.

Let us *cure* them. The poet who mistakes a real woman for his Muse and acts accordingly. . . . The young man who sets off in a yacht in search of God. . . .

The outer divorced from any illumination from the inner is in a state of darkness. We are in an age of darkness. The state of outer darkness is a state of sin – i.e.

116

alienation or estrangement from the *inner light*.* Certain actions lead to greater estrangement; certain others help one not to be so far removed. The former used to be called sinful.

The ways of losing one's way are legion. Madness is certainly not the least unambiguous. The counter-madness of Kraepelinian psychiatry is the exact counterpart of 'official' psychosis. Literally, and absolutely seriously, it is as *mad*, if by madness we mean any radical estrangement from the totality of what is the case. Remember Kierkegaard's objective madness.

As we experience the world, so we act. We conduct ourselves in the light of our view of what is the case and what is not the case. That is, each person is a more or less naïve ontologist. Each person has views of what is, and what is not.

There is no doubt, it seems to me, that there have been profound changes in the experience of man in the last thousand years. In some ways this is more evident than changes in the patterns of his behaviour. There is everything to suggest that man experienced God. Faith was never a matter of believing he existed, but of trusting in the Presence that was experienced and known to exist as a self-validating datum. It seems likely that far more people in our time neither experience the Presence of God, nor the Presence of his absence, but the absence of his Presence.

We require a history of phenomena; not simply more phenomena of history.

As it is, the secular psychotherapist is often in the role of the blind leading the half-blind.

The fountain has not played itself out, the flame still

* M. Eliade, *The Two and the One* (London: Harvill Press, 1965) especially Chapter I.

shines, the river still flows, the spring still bubbles forth, the light has not faded. But between *us* and It there is a veil which is more like fifty feet of solid concrete. *Deus absconditus*. Or we have absconded.

Already everything in our time is directed to categorizing and segregating this reality from objective facts. This is precisely the concrete wall. Intellectually, emotionally, inter-personally, organizationally, intuitively, theoretically, we have to blast our way through the solid wall, even if at the risk of chaos, madness and death. For from *this* side of the wall, this is the risk. There are no assurances, no guarantees.

Many people are prepared to have faith in the sense of scientifically indefensible belief in an untested hypothesis. Few have trust enough to test it. Many people make-believe what they experience. Few are made to believe by their experience. Paul of Tarsus was picked up by the scruff of the neck, thrown to the ground and blinded for three days. This direct experience was self-validating.

We live in a secular world. To adapt to this world the child abdicates its ecstasy. ('*L'enfant abdique son extase*': Mallarmé.) Having lost our experience of the spirit, we are expected to have faith. But this faith comes to be a belief in a reality which is not evident. There is a prophecy in Amos that there will be a time when there will be a famine in the land, 'not a famine for bread, nor a thirst for water, but of *hearing* the words of the Lord.' That time has now come to pass. It is the present age.

From the alienated starting point of our pseudo-sanity, everything is equivocal. Our sanity is not 'true' sanity. Their madness is not 'true' madness. The madness of our patients is an artefact of the destruction wreaked on them by us, and by them on themselves. Let no one suppose that we meet 'true' madness any more than that we are

118

truly sane. The madness that we encounter in 'patients' is a gross travesty, a mockery, a grotesque caricature of what the natural healing of that estranged integration we call sanity might be. True sanity entails in one way or another the dissolution of the normal ego, that false self competently adjusted to our alienated social reality: the emergence of the 'inner' archetypal mediators of divine power, and through this death a rebirth, and the eventual re-establishment of a new kind of ego-functioning, the ego now being the servant of the divine, no longer its betrayer.

Chapter 7

A Ten-Day Voyage

JESSE WATKINS is now a well-known sculptor. I am glad
to know him as a friend.

He was born 31 December 1899. Went to sea in 1916
on a tramp steamer during World War I. His first trip was
to North Russia. In the same year he was torpedoed in
the Mediterranean. In 1932 he served in a square-rigged
sailing ship.

He ended the Second World War (during which he
served in the Royal Navy) as a Commander and Com-
modore of coastal convoys. During his career at sea he
encountered shipwreck, mutiny and murder.

He has drawn and painted since early youth and constantly did so at sea. While ashore for brief periods he
attended sporadically life classes at Goldsmiths' College
and Chelsea Art School. He has also written and had
published short stories of the sea.

Twenty-seven years ago Watkins went through a
'psychotic episode' that lasted ten days. I tape-recorded a
discussion with him about it in 1964 and with his per-
mission extracts are presented here.

The material speaks for itself. It is an account of his
voyage into inner space and time. Its general features are
not unusual, but it is unusual to have such a lucid account of them. Although the events are twenty-seven
years old, they are vivid in his mind and constitute one of
the most significant experiences of his life.

The preliminaries

Before his Voyage began, Jesse had 'moved into an
entirely new environment'. He had been working seven

days a week, until late at night. He felt physically, emotionally, spiritually at a 'low ebb'. Since it is the voyage itself that we are concerned with here, we shall not go into the antecedent circumstances in more detail. Then he was bitten by a dog, and the wound did not heal. He went to hospital where he was given a general anaesthetic for the first time in his life and had the wound dressed.

He returned home by bus and sat down in a chair. His son aged seven came into the room and Jesse saw him in a new and strange way, somehow unremoved from himself.

Then it began.

The voyage

' . . . suddenly I looked at the clock and the wireless was on and then the music was playing – um – oh, popular sort of bit of music. It was based on the rhythm of a tram. Taa-ta-ta-taa-taa – something like Ravel's repetitive tune. And then when that happened I suddenly felt as if time was going back. I felt this time going back, I had this extraordinary feeling of – er – that was the greatest feeling I had at that moment was of time going backwards. . . .

'I even felt it so strongly I looked at the clock and in some way I felt that the clock was reinforcing my own opinion of time going back although I couldn't see the hands moving – – – I felt alarmed because I suddenly felt as if I was moving somewhere on a kind of conveyor belt – and unable to do anything about it, as if I was slipping along and sliding down a – shute as it were and – er – unable to stop myself. And – um – this gave me a rather panicky feeling – – – I remember going into the other room in order to see where I was, to look at my own face, and there were no mirrors in that room. I went into the other room, and I looked into the mirror at myself, and I looked in a way strange, I seemed as though I were looking at someone who – someone who was familiar but – er – very strange and different from myself – as I felt – – and then I had extraordinary feelings that I was quite capable of doing anything with myself, that I had a feeling of being in control of – of all my faculties, body and everything else, – – and I started rambling on.'

One sees the old and familiar in a new and strange way. Often as though for the first time. One's old moorings are lost. One goes back in time. One is embarked on the oldest voyage in the world.

'My wife became very – um – worried. She came in and told me to sit down and lie down in bed and because she was alarmed she got hold of the man next door to come in. He was a civil servant and he was also a bit alarmed and he calmed me down, and I was rambling on to him, and the doctor came up – um – and I was talking of a lot of these feelings I had in my mind about time going back. Of course, to me they sounded perfectly rational, I was going back and thinking that I was going back into sort of previous existences, but only vaguely. And they obviously looked at me as if I were mad, I could feel – I could see the look in their faces and I felt it was not much good talking to them because they obviously thought that I was quite round the bend, as I might have been. And – um – then the next thing was that an ambulance came and I was taken off. . . .'

He was taken to an observation ward.

'I was put into bed and – um – – well, I remember that night it was an appalling sort of experience because I had the – had the feeling that – um – that I was then – that I had died. And I felt that other people were in beds around me, and I thought they were all other people that had died – and they were there – just waiting to pass on to the next department . . .'

He had not died physically, but his 'ego' had died. Along with this ego-loss, this death, came feelings of the enhanced significance and relevance of everything.

Loss of ego may be confused with physical death. Projected images of one's own mind may be experienced as persecutors. One's own ego-less mind may be confused with one's ego. And so on. Under such circumstances a person may panic, become paranoid, with ideas of reference and influence, become inflated with ideas of grandeur, etc.

Some confusion of this kind need not be alarming. But who can say that he is entirely unafraid to die, or, if he searches his heart even further, that he feels entitled to die?

' . . . then I started going into this – – real feeling of regression in time. I had quite extraordinary feelings of – living, not only *living*, but – er – feeling and – er – experiencing everything relating to something I felt that was – well, something like animal life and so on. At one time I actually seemed to be wandering in a kind of landscape with – um – desert landscape – as if I were an animal, rather – rather a large animal. It sounds absurd to say so but I felt as if I were a kind of rhinoceros or something like that and emitting sounds like a rhinoceros and being at the same time afraid and at the same time being aggressive and on guard. And then – um – going back to further periods of regression and even sort of when I was just struggling like something that had no brain at all and as if I were just struggling for my own existence against other things which were opposing me. And – um – then at times I felt as if I were like a baby – I could even – I – I could even hear myself cry like a child. . . .

'All these feelings were very acute and – um – real and, and at the same time I was – I had – I was aware of them, you know, I've got the memory of them still. I was aware of these things happening to me – in some vague sort of way, I was a sort of observer of myself but yet experiencing it. I had all kinds of feelings of – this sounds, because it's nearly thirty years since I experienced it, it sounds a bit disjointed because I've got to drag it out of my memory but I want to be particular that I'm only telling exactly what happened to me and not embellishing it with any sort of imagination or anything like that. Um – I found that I had periods when I came right out of this state, that I'd been sort of moving into, and then comparatively lucid states I had, but I was reading – I read newspapers, because they gave me newspapers and things to read, but I couldn't read them because everything that I read had a large number of associations with it. I mean I'd just read a headline and the headline of this item of news would have – have quite sort of – very much wider associations in my mind. It seemed to start off everything I read and everything that sort of caught my attention seemed to start off everything I read and everything that sort of caught my attention seemed to start off, bang-bang-bang, like that with an enormous number of associations moving off into things so that it became so difficult for me to deal with that I couldn't read. Everything seemed to have a much greater – very much greater significance than normally. I had a letter from my wife. I remember the letter she wrote to me and she said, "The sun is shining

here" – and – er – "It's a nice day." This is one of the
phrases in the letter. There were a number of other
phrases and I can't remember all of them and I can't remember all of the phrases in the letter which evoked
responses in me, but I remember this one. She said "The
sun is shining here." And I felt that if it were – that this
was a letter from *her*, she was in a quite different world.
She was in a world that I could never inhabit any more, –
and this gave me feelings of alarm and I felt somehow that
I was – I'd gone off into a world that I could never move
out of.'

Although out of the safe harbour of one's own identity
anchored in this time and this place, the traveller may
still be clearly aware of this time and place *as well*.

'You know, I was perfectly well aware of myself and
aware of the surroundings.'

Jesse felt he had enhanced powers of control over his
body and could affect others.

'. . . when I went to the hospital, because of this feeling,
this intense feeling of being able to – um – govern myself,
my body and so on, I said to the nurse who wanted to
bandage my finger up: "You needn't bother about that."
I took the thing off and I said: "That'll be all right to-
morrow if you don't deal with it at all and just leave it."
And I remember I had this terrific feeling that I could do
this and – this was – this was a nasty cut right down my
finger. I wouldn't allow them to put anything on it and
they said, oh well, it's not bleeding and they'd leave it, and
the next day it was perfectly healed up, and because – it
sort of – I put a sort of intense – er – attention on it in

order to make it do that. I found that I – I tested myself with the man opposite me in this ward who was very noisy at times, he used to get out of his bed, he'd been having a number of nasty abdominal operations and I suppose it had affected him and probably had caused his breakdown. But he used to get up out of bed and swear and shout and so on, and I felt a bit alarmed about him and I felt very compassionate towards him, and I used to sit in my bed and make him lie down by sort of looking at him and thinking about it, and he used to lie down. And to try to see whether this – this was a – just an accident, I had tried it also with another patient at the same time and I found that he – that I could make him lie down.'

I would not too readily discount these possibilities.

'I felt that I had sort of – um – tapped powers that I in some vague way I had felt I had, or everybody had, although at that time I'd been a sailor most of my life, I had not – I had read quite a bit when I'd been at sea but I hadn't read any esoteric literature then nor had I since, I hadn't read anything to do with, er – with – ideas of trans-mog-migration of souls or whatever you call it, trans-mog – transmig – reincarnation. But I had a feeling at times of an enormous journey in front, quite, – er – a fantastic journey, and it seemed that I had got an under-standing of things which I'd been trying to understand for a long time, problems of good and evil and so on, and that I had solved it in as much that I had come to the conclusion, with all the feelings that I had at the time, that I was more – more than I had always imagined myself, not just existing now, but I had existed since the very begin-ning – er – in a kind of – from the lowest form of life to the present time, and that that was the sum of my real experiences, and that what I was doing was experiencing them again. And that then, occasionally, I had this sort of vista ahead of me as though I was looking down – looking to an enormous – or rather all the – not *looking* so much as just feeling – ahead of me was lying the most horrific journey, the only way I can describe it is a journey – a journey to – um – to the final sort of business of – um – being aware of all – everything, and that – and the – and I felt this so strongly, it was such a horrifying experience to suddenly feel that, that I immediately shut myself off from it because I couldn't contemplate it, because it sort of shivered me up. I – it drove me into a state of fear, so much – I was unable to take it.'

'Of the task that was still ahead?'

'Yes, the – that was the enormity of it, that I – that there was no way of avoiding this – facing up to what I – the journey I had to do. I had, I suppose because of having been brought up in the religious atmosphere, I had – my mother's religious, not in the church sort of way but religious in a – in a real sort of way, tried to teach us something about religion and – er – the sort of attitude to life. . . .'

He had a 'particularly acute feeling' that things were divided into three levels: an antechamber level, a central world, and a higher world. Most people were waiting in the antechamber to get into the next department, which was what he had now entered:

'. . . they were sort of awakening. I was also aware of a – um – a higher sphere, as it were. I mean, I'm rather chary of using some of these phrases because they're used so many times – you know, people talk about spheres and all that sort of thing, but – er – the only thing that I felt – and when I'm describing these things I'm describing more feelings – er – a deeper experience than just looking at the thing . . . an awareness of – um – of another sphere, another layer of existence lying above the – not only the antechamber but the present – lying above the two of them, a sort of three-layered – um – existence. . . .'

'What was the lowest one?'

'The lowest one was just a kind of waiting – like a waiting room.'

This was linked to the experience of time.

'I wasn't just living on the – the moving moment, the present, but I was moving and living in a – in another time dimension added to the time situation in which I am now. . . . The point I want to make is that I hadn't got any ideology. The only ideological part of what I told you was the part where I went through the Stations of the Cross, because there I was sort of joining it up with an ideology at that time. I have often thought about what I went through then. I tried to make some sort of – um – sense out of it because I feel that it was not senseless – although I suppose to others about me I was – er – mad in as much as I was not living in this present time, and if I was not living in this present time I was therefore incapable of coping with it properly. But I had this feeling all the time of – er – moving back – even backwards and forwards in time, that I was not just living in the present moment. And I could much more easily go back than I could go forward because the forward movement was a bit too much for me to take.'

Such an experience can be extremely confusing and may end disastrously. There are no guarantees. Jesse experienced three planes of reality instead of the usual one. Apart from going through the Stations of the Cross he did not link up with any ideology. He had no map.

But he trusted his experience of having entered into a state of more, not less, reality, of *hyper*-sanity, not sub-sanity. To others, these two possibilities may be no more distinguishable from each other than chalk from cheese. He had to be careful.

'I had feelings of – er – of gods, not only God but gods as it were, of beings which are far above us capable of – er – dealing with the situation that I was incapable of dealing with, that were in charge and were running things and – um – at the end of it, everybody had to take on the job at the top. And it was this business that made it such a devastating thing to contemplate, that at some period in the existence of – er – of oneself one had to take on this job, even for only a momentary period, because you had arrived then at awareness of everything. What was beyond that I don't know. At the time I felt that – um – that God himself was a madman . . . because he's got this enormous load of having to be aware and governing and running things – um – and that all of us had to come up and finally get to the point where we had to experience that ourselves. . . . I know that sounds completely crazy to you but that's what I sort of felt at the time.'

'You mean a "madman" in the sense that people in the state that you were in are taken to be mad?'

'Yes, that's what I meant, that he was – er – he was mad. Everything below him or everything below that got to the point where he got – er – had to treat him like that because he was the one that was taking it all at that moment – and that the – er – the journey is there and every single one of us has got to go through it, and – um –

everything – you can't dodge it. . . . the purpose of everything and the whole of existence is – er – to equip you to
take another step, and another step, and another step, and
so on. . . .'

Jesse felt that this experience was a stage that everyone
would have to go through one way or another in order to
reach a higher stage of evolution.

' . . . it's an experience that – um – we have at some
stage to go through, but that was only one – and that –
many more – a fantastic number of – um – things have
got to impinge upon us until we gradually build ourselves
up into an acceptance of reality, and a greater and greater
acceptance of reality and what really exists – and that any
dodging of it could only – delays the time and it's just as if
you were going to sea in a boat that was not really capable
of dealing with the storms that can rise.'

Eventually he felt he couldn't 'take' any more. He
decided to come back.

'The nurse told me that sometimes I kept them awake
at night by talking. And they – they put me into a padded
cell and I said, "Well, don't put me in here," I said, you
know, I said, "I can't bear it." But they said, "But you –
we've got to try to do it because you make such a noise
you know – talking." So they put me into this place and I
said, "Well, leave the door open", so they left the door
open, and I remember going through that night struggling with – with something that wanted to – some sort of
– curiosity or willingness to open myself to – um – experiencing – this, and the panic and the insufficiency of
spirit that would enable me to experience it. And during

that time I went through – I went through the Stations of the Cross, although I'd never been what you might call a really religious person – I'm not now – and I went through all that sort of – those sort of feelings. Well the – all this experience became – went on for quite a time and I began to – they kept on giving me sedatives to make me sleep, and I – one morning I decided that I was not going to take any more sedatives, and that I had got to stop this business going on because I couldn't cope with it any more....'

The return

'I sat on the bed, and I thought, well, somewhere or other I've got to sort of join up with my present – er – self, very strongly. So I sat on the bed, I clenched my hands together tightly. And the nurse had just been along and said to me, "Well, I want you to take this", and I said, "I'm not taking any more because I should – the more I take of that the less capable I am of doing anything now – I mean – as I said, I shall go under." And so I sat on the bed and I held my hands together, and as – I suppose in a clumsy way of linking myself up with my present self, I kept on saying my own name over and over again and all of a sudden, just like that – I suddenly realized that it was all over. All the experiences were finished, and it was a dramatic – a dramatic ending to it all. And there was a doctor there who had been a naval – a rear admiral surgeon – surgeon rear admiral, and he and I had become friendly because we talked about the sea from time to time. And this nurse came along and said, "You haven't drunk that", and I said, "I told you I'm not drinking it", and he said, "Well, I'll have to go and get the doctor", and I said, "Well, you get the doctor." Then the doctor came along and I said, "I don't want any more of that sedative," I said, "I'm quite capable of – of running things normally now," I said, "I'm all right." And he looked at me and he looked at my eyes and he said, "Oh," he said, "I can see that." And he laughed, and that's what happened, and from that moment I had – never had any more of these feelings. . . .'

Jesse came through it.

'But at times it was so – um – devastating, and it taxed my spirit to the limit, that I'd be afraid of entering it again. . . .

'I was . . . suddenly confronted with something so much greater than oneself, with so many more experiences, with so much awareness, so much that you couldn't take it. It's as if something soft were dropped into a bag of nails. . . .

'I didn't have the capacity for experiencing it. I experienced it for a moment or two but it was like a sudden blast of light, wind, or whatever you like to put it as, against you so that you feel that you're too naked and alone to be able to withstand it, you're not strong enough. It's like a child or an animal suddenly confronted – or being aware of – an adult's experiences for him, for instance. The grown-up person has experienced a lot in their life time, they've built up gradually their capacity for experiencing life and looking at things – and – er – understanding them, even experiencing them for all kinds of reasons, for aesthetic reasons, for artistic reasons, for religious reasons, for all kinds of reasons we experience things, which for – if a child or an animal, say, were suddenly confronted with these things they couldn't take it because they're not strong enough, they haven't got the equipment to do it. And I was facing things then that I just hadn't got the equipment to deal with. I was too soft, I was too vulnerable.'

A person in this state may be 'difficult' for others, especially when the whole experience is being conducted in the quite bizarrely incongruous context of mental hospitals as they are at present. The true physician-priest would enable people to have such experiences before they are driven to extremities. Does one have to be dying of malnutrition before one is allowed a meal? Jesse Watkins was, however, luckier than many patients would now be, in that he appears to have been sedated comparatively lightly, and was not given any 'treatment' in the forms of electro shocks, deep-freezing, etc.

Instead, he was simply put in a padded cell if he was too much for the others.

If Jesse had had to cope with 'modern' forms of psychiatric 'treatment' as well, it would probably have been too much for him.

' . . . I would have to – I felt as if I would give in and that I wouldn't want to be aware of anything at all and I'd just sort of coil up and – um – stop existing as it were. I felt that I couldn't take any more because I'd been through such – been through such an awful lot, and I suppose there comes a point where a person can only take so much and then they give up because they just can't take it any more. And if I couldn't have taken it any more I should have – I don't know what might have happened – perhaps a feeling of sudden cessation and everything, and if – if they had done that to me I don't know what I would have been able to – how I would have been able to cope with it, not being shut in that room and – er – of course the room itself, I mean, with the brown, padded walls and floor and all that. . . .'

I asked him what principles he felt should underly the care provided during such a voyage.

' . . . you are like a vessel in a storm. It puts out a sheet anchor which helps the boat to weather the storm because it keeps its head to the wind, but it also gives it a feeling of comfort – er – to those aboard the boat, to think they've got a sheet anchor that's not attached to the bottom but it's a part of the sea, that – er – enables them to survive, and then as long as they think they're going to survive as a boat then they can go through experiencing the storm. Gradually they begin to – they feel quite happy with it even though the sheet anchor might have broken adrift and so on. I feel that if ever a person were to – ever to experience that sort of thing, he's got to have – well, one hand for himself, as it were, and one hand for the experience. He's not going to be able to – I think, if he's going to survive – to get away from his present level where he is . . . because of all that has gone before, and there's gradually been a building up of – er – the necessary equipment to deal with the present situation for himself. And that he's not equipped for anything more than that, not very much. Some people are equipped more for it and some are less – but he's got to have some way, some sort of sheet anchor which is holding on to the present – and to himself as he is – to be able to experience even a little bit of what he's got to experience.'

'So there should be other people who sort of look after you. . . .'

'Other people who you trust and who know that you are to be looked after, that they won't let you go adrift and sink. It's – um – just a question of – you see I feel that – that this business of experiencing is a matter of one's building up one's own spirit. Because I remember – to take a normal analogy – of when I went to sea first I was a little boy of sixteen, and we went up to the north of Russia, and we experienced some quite extraordinary storms when the sea was washing over the ship and the ship was rolling terrifically, and there was no food, and I had never experienced anything like this in my life before. Because I'd never even been to a boarding school, I'd been at home, I'd been to a day school and never been far away from my mother. And the sudden impact of this rough and terrific fear-invoking life was a bit more than I could take at the time – and – but then, gradually, as I went into it more, then I first of all started sort of – by being – or pretending to be brave. Then I gradually began to stand up to it, and the thing that gave me comfort sometimes was the fact that other people were taking it, they were living in this – er – environment and they appeared to be quite all right. They gave me no sympathy, you had no sympathy from anybody, and you were left on your own – er – resources to stand up to it. And I stood up to it and then, of course, looking back over the years I can remember sometimes when I had been quite afraid of very big storms at sea – um – but I thought – I often thought when I'd been through these storms I was equipped to deal with them then from experience – but I often thought back to those times when I was a little boy, when I first went to sea, the first week, – because during the first week I was at sea, we went through quite an extraordinary gale, wind, when the galley was washed out, there was no food, and everything was wet, and the ship was rolling about and we were in danger of being shipwrecked and so on – er – I was stricken with fear simply because I hadn't got the equipment to deal with it. And that's I suppose the nearest I can take in analogy of how I felt then, was – er – this suddenly faced with this – enormity of knowing. . . .

' . . . I think that – er – ten days and what I went through then, it certainly pushed me on quite a bit. And I re-

135

member when I came out of hospital, I was there for about three months altogether, when I came out I suddenly felt that everything was so much more real that it – than it had been before. The grass was greener, the sun was shining brighter, and people were more alive, I could see them clearer. I could see the bad things and the good things and all that. I was much more aware.'

There is a great deal that urgently needs to be written about this and similar experiences. But I am going to confine myself to a few matters of fundamental orientation.

We can no longer assume that such a voyage is an illness that has to be treated. Yet the padded cell is now outdated by the 'improved' methods of treatment now in use.

If we can demystify ourselves, we see 'treatment' (electro-shocks, tranquillizers, deep-freezing – sometimes even psychoanalysis) as ways of stopping this sequence from occurring.

Can we not see that *this voyage is not what we need to be cured of, but that it is itself a natural way of healing our own appalling state of alienation called normality*?

In other times people intentionally embarked upon this voyage.

Or if they found themselves already embarked, willy-nilly, they gave thanks, as for a special grace.

Today, some people still set out. But perhaps the majority find themselves forced out of the 'normal' world by being placed in an untenable position in it. They have no *orientation** in the geography of inner space and time, and are likely to get lost very quickly without a guide.

* Orientation means to know where the orient is. For inner space, to know the east, the origin or source of our experience.

In Chapter 5 I listed different features of such a journey. They seem to fit Jesse Watkins' experience quite well. (When Jesse gave me this account, we had not had any prior discussions on this subject, and he had not read anything I had written.) But this is still only a tentative approximation.* Jung broke the ground here, but few have followed him.

One would hope that society will set up places whose express purpose would be to help people through the stormy passages of such a voyage. A considerable part of this book has been devoted to showing why this is unlikely.

In this particular type of journey, the direction we have to take is *back* and *in*, because it was way back that we started to go down and out. They will say we are regressed and withdrawn and out of contact with them. True enough, we have a long, long way to go back to contact the reality we have all long lost contact with. And because they are humane, and concerned, and even love us, and are very frightened, they will try to cure us. They may succeed. But there is still hope that they will fail.

---

* For a beautifully lucid, autobiographical description of a psychotic episode that lasted six months, and whose healing function is clear, see Barbara O'Brien, *Operators and Things* (London: Elek Books Ld, 1958).

The Bird of Paradise

Jesus said to them:

When you make the two one, and
when you make the inner as the outer
and the outer as the inner and the above
as the below, and when
you make the male and female into a single one,
so that the male will not be male and
the female not be female, when you make
eyes in the place of an eye, and a hand
in the place of a hand, and a foot in the place
of a foot, and an image in the place of an image,
then shall you enter the Kingdom.

The Gospel According to Thomas

Each night I meet him. King with Crown. Each night we fight. Why must he kill me? No. I shall not die. I can be smaller than a pinhead, harder than a diamond. Suddenly, how gentle he is! One of his tricks. Off with his Crown! Strike. Bash in his skull. Face streams of blood. Tears? Perhaps. Too late! Off with his head! Pith the spine! Die now, O King!

Spider-crab moves slowly across bedroom wall. Not horrible, not evil. Acceptance. Another one appears and another. Ugh! No, too much. Kill.

Suddenly it was always a bird, so frail, so beautiful: now, twitching in death agony. What have I done? But why play such a game on me? Why appear so ugly. It's your fault, your fault.

Noon. Traffic jam. At first I can't make out why. Then I see. A large, magnificent dog is wandering in aimless circles across the road. It wanders closer to my car. I begin to realize that there is something terribly damaged about it. Yes, back broken, and as it veers round, the left face comes into view – bashed-in, bloody, formless, mess, on which its eye lies somehow intact, looking at me, with no socket, just by itself, alone, detached. A crowd has gathered, laughing, jeering, at the ridiculous behaviour of this distracted creature. Motorists hoot their horns and shout at it to get out of the way. Shop girls have come out of their shops and giggle together.

Can I be that dog and those angry motorists and those giggling shop girls?

Is Christ forgiving me for crucifying Him?

Glasgow.
Grey street. Blank faceless tenements
streaming with my drizzle. Red only in
children's cheeks. Light fading from
still laughing eyes. . . .

Glasgow repartee

FELLA (*to passing bird*): Hey, hen – yi'll heat yir water.
BIRD: You're no going tae dip yir wick in it onyway.

Those termini of Glasgow tramcars in the 1930s in
November Sunday afternoon. The end.
Flaking plaster. Broken window panes.
The smell of slum tenements. The dank 'closes' on a
Sunday morning.
Impregnated with stale beer, vomit, fish and chips.

All that floral wallpaper and those borders, the curtains
and the blinds. The three-piece uncut moquette.
The tiled fireplaces, the fireguards, the acres and acres
of mock parquet linoleum.

The tiled close with banister and the stained glass
window. The respectability. O the respectability.

Mrs Campbell was a nice young mother of two children. She had rather suddenly started to lose weight, and
her abdomen had begun to swell. But she did not feel too
ill in herself.
The medical student has to 'take a history of the illness' – I made the mistake of chatting with her, learning

about her little boy and her little girl, what she was knitting, and so on.

She came into our surgical ward on a Sunday. A mark was placed on her abdomen to show where the lower border of her liver was, because it was enlarged.

On Monday her liver had grown further down. Even cancer can't grow at that rate. She was evidently suffering from something very unusual.

Her liver continued to grow every day. By Thursday it was clear she was going to die. She did not know this – and no one dreamt of telling her.

'We've decided you don't need an operation.'

'When will I be going home then?'

'Well perhaps in a little while, but we still have to keep you under observation.'

'But will I be getting any treatment?'

'Don't worry, Mrs Campbell, leave it to us. We still have some investigations to do yet.'

She probably had a haemorrhage going on inside her liver. But why? Secondary growths from a cancer somewhere? But where? Every part of her body had been probed, palpated, up her rectum, vagina – down her throat, X-rayed, urine, faeces, blood. . . . It was an interesting clinical problem.

On Friday morning the students met with one of the young surgeons and her case was discussed. No one had seen such a case – we would find out at the post-mortem of course, but it would be nice if we could hit the diagnosis beforehand.

Someone suggested a small tumour in her retina. Her eyes had been looked into – but these tumours are sometimes very small indeed, easy to miss – when she had been first examined this wasn't being looked for specifically – perhaps – it was a long shot. It was almost lunchtime – at lunchtime over five hundred students ran from their classes all over the university buildings to the students' Refectory – where there was seating for two hundred. If you didn't get at the top of the queue you would have to wait an hour or more, and you only had an hour before the next lecture.

But we just had time to dash up to look into her eyes. . . .

When we got to her the nurses were already laying her out, tying up her ankles.

Fuck it, she's dead! Still, quickly, before the cornea clouds over. We looked into the depths of her dead eyes. Dead only a few minutes after all. If you look into eyes at that time it's interesting anyway – you see the blood actually beginning to break up in the veins of the retina. But apart from that, nothing to see.

Fuck her, we've missed our fucking lunch.

Bookshop, Glasgow. Usual copy of *Horizon*. The last number!

'It is closing time now in the Gardens of the West. From now on a writer will be judged by the resonances of his silence and the quality of his despair.'

All right – you did not have a circulation of more than eighty thousand. You ran out of money. But you bastard, speak for yourself. Write *Horizon* off and wish yourself off. Don't write me off. I'll be judged by my music not by my silence and by the quality of whatever pathetic shreds of faith, hope and charity still cling to me.

AMERICAN SAILOR (*to Glasgow Hairy*): Baby, I'm going to give you something you've never had before.
GLASGOW HAIRY (*to friend*): Hey, Maggie. There's a guy here with leprosy.

Fifty cadavers laid out on slabs. Before we are finished we shall each have got to know one of them intimately.

At the end of that term when they had all been dissected to bits – suddenly, – so it seemed – no one knew how it began – pieces of skin, muscle, penises, bits of liver, lung, heart, tongue, etc. etc. were all flying about, shouts, screams. Who was fighting whom? God knows.

The professor had been standing in the doorway for some while before his presence began to creep through the room. Silence.

'You should be ashamed of yourselves,' he thundered; 'how do you expect them to sort themselves out on the Day of Judgement?'

He was ten years of age and had hydrocephalus due to an inoperable tumour the size of a very small pea, just at the right place to stop his cerebrospinal fluid from getting out of his head, which is to say that he had water on the brain, that was bursting his head, so that the brain was becoming stretched out into a thinning rim, and his skull bones likewise. He was in excruciating and unremitting pain.

One of my jobs was to put a long needle into this ever-increasing fluid to let it out. I had to do this twice a day, and the so-clear fluid that was killing him would leap out at me from his massive ten-year-old head, rising in a brief column to several feet, sometimes hitting my face.

Cases like this are usually less distressing than they might be, because they are often heavily doped, they partially lose their faculties, sometimes an operation helps. He had had several, but the new canal that was made didn't work.

The condition can sometimes be stabilized at the level of being a chronic vegetable for indefinite years – so that the person finally does not seem to suffer. (Do not despair, the soul dies even before the body.)

But this little boy unmistakably endured agony. He would quietly cry in pain. If he would only have shrieked or complained. . . . And he knew he was going to die.

He had started reading *The Pickwick Papers*. The one thing he asked God for, he told me, was that he be allowed to finish this book before he died.

He died before it was half-finished.

I know so many bad jokes. At least I didn't invent them.

Jimmy McKenzie was a bloody pest at the mental hospital because he went around shouting back at his voices. We could only hear one end of the conversation, of course, but the other end could be inferred in general terms at least from:

'Away tae fuck, ye filthy-minded bastards. . . .'

It was decided at one and the same time to alleviate his distress and ours, by giving him the benefit of a leucotomy.

An improvement in his condition was noted.

After the operation he went around no longer shouting abuse at his voices, but: 'What's that? Say that again! Speak up ye buggers, I cannae hear ye!'

We had been attending a childbirth and it had dragged on and off for sixteen hours. Finally it started to come – grey, slimy, cold – out it came – a large human frog – an anencephalic monster, no neck, no head, with eyes, nose, froggy mouth, long arms.

This creature was born at 9.10 a.m. on a clear August morning.

Maybe it was slightly alive. We didn't want to know. We wrapped it in newspaper – and with this bundle under my arm to take back to the pathology lab., that seemed to cry out for all the answerable answers that I ever asked, I walked along O'Connell Street two hours later.

THE BIRD OF PARADISE

I needed a drink. I went into a pub, put the bundle on the bar. Suddenly the desire, to unwrap it, hold it up for all to see, a ghastly Gorgon's head, to turn the world to stone.

I could show you the exact spot on the pavement to this day.

Fingertips, legs, lungs, genitals, all thinking.

These people in the street are there, I see them. We are told they are something out there, that traverses space, hits eyes, goes to brain, then an event occurs whereby this event in my brain is experienced by me as those people out there in space.

The I that I am is not the me that I know, but the wherewith and whereby the *me* is known. But if this I that is the wherewith and whereby is not anything that I know, then it is no thing – nothing. Click – sluice gates open – body guts outside in.

Head with legs sings merrily in the streets, led along by a beggar. The head is an egg. A stupid old woman prises open the egg-head. Foetus. Its singing is its cries of unspeakable agony. The old woman sets fire to the foetus. It turns inside the egg-head as though in a frying pan. Commotion. Its agony and helplessness is indescribable. I am burning, I can't move. There are cries, 'It's dead!' But the doctor pronounces that it's still alive and orders it to be taken to a hospital.

Two men sit facing each other and both of them are me. Quietly, meticulously, systematically, they are blowing out each other's brains, with pistols. They look perfectly intact. Inside devastation.

I look round a New Town. What a pity about those viscera and abortions littering the new spick and span gutters. This one looks like a heart. It is pulsating. It starts to move on four little legs. It is disgusting and grotesque. Dog-like abortion of raw red flesh, and yet alive. Stupid, flayed, abortive dog still persisting in living. Yet all it asks after all is that I let it love me, and not even that.

Astonished heart, loving unloved heart, heart of a heartless world, crazy heart of a dying world.

Playing the game of reality with no real cards in one's hand.

Body mangled, torn into shreds, ground down to powder, limbs aching, heart lost, bones pulverized, empty nausea in dust. Wanting to vomit up my lungs. Everywhere blood, tissues, muscles, bones, are wild, frantic. Outwardly all is quiet, calm, as ever. Sleep. Death. I look all right.

That wild silent screech in the night. And what if I were to tear my hair and run naked and screaming through the suburban night. I would wake up a few tired people and get myself committed to a mental hospital. To what purpose?

5.00 a.m.: Vultures hover outside my window.

Majestic forest, hot summer's day. Proud trees, well rooted in earth, scraping heaven, tall, powerful. A forest at its grandest.

The woodcutters come. They saw and hack down the trees. Who can endure or escape the agony of those saws. The trees are felled – processed in sawmills, sawn down and down and down, finally to sawdust, finer and finer grained, less and less and less, dissolving into the stuff of all the world.

The Lotus opens. Movement from earth, through water, from fire to air. Out and in beyond life and death now, beyond inner and outer, sense and non-sense, meaning and futility, male and female, being and non-being, light and darkness, void and plenum. Beyond all duality, or non-duality, beyond and beyond. Disincarnation. I breathe again.

The farther *in*, large or small, the more and less there is, more and more nothing, further into the atom, further out into space, nothing. The Portal of the Last Judgement of Autun and the centre of an atom are identical. Jumping Jesus. Ecstasy. Cosmic froth and bubbles of perpetual movement of Creation Redemption Resurrection Judgement Last and First and Ultimate Beginning and End are One Mandala of Atom Flower of Christ. The eye of the needle is here and now. Two heartbeats enlace infinity. What we know is froth and bubbles.

Light. Light of the World, that irradiates me and shines through my eyes. Inner sun that emblazons me, brighter than ten thousand suns.

Terror of being blinded, frizzled up, destroyed. Clutch at myself. Fall. Fall away from Light to Darkness, from the Kingdom into exile, from Eternity to time, from Heaven to earth. Away, away, away and out, down and out, through and past winds of other worlds, spiral energy dance – through and past galaxies of stars, colours, gems, through and past the beginnings of contentions. The fingers of the one hand begin to fight one another. Beginnings of gods – each level of being longing now for the lower – gods fighting and fucking themselves into incarnation. Demigods, heroes, mortal men. Carnage. Butchery of spirit in final horror of incarnation. Blood. Agony. Exhaustion of spirit. Struggle between death and rebirth, enervation and regeneration.

Cosmic vomit, sperm, smegma, diarrhoea, sweat – at all events, an insignificant particle on the way out. . . .

The vision has ended, I am starting to dream again. Concussed. Fragmented scraps of memory. Poor raw, smashed Egg Head. A time haemorrhage in the body of Eternity.

Beginning to *think* again – to grasp, to connect, to put together, to remember. . . .

Only to remember to remember, or at least remember you have forgotten. . . .

Each forgetting a dismembering.

I must never forget again. All that searching and re-searching those false signposts, the terrible danger of forgetting that one has forgotten. It's too awful.

Behind above beyond and in man the war rages on. Man, me and you, is not the only site of the battle, but he is one region of it. Mind and body are torn, ripped, shredded, ravaged, exhausted by these Powers and Principalities in their cosmic conflict that we cannot even identify.

We are shattered, tattered, demented remnants of a once-glorious army. Among us are Princes, and Captains of Armies, Lords of Battles, amnesic, aphasic, ataxic, jerkily trying to recall what was the battle the sounds of which still ring in our ears – is the battle still raging? If we could only make contact with Headquarters, only make our way back to join the main body of the Army. . . .

A soldier on the Wall at the furthest reaches of the Empire – looking out towards the darkness and danger. The next nearest comrade is out of sight. I must not desert – I will be recalled to the Capital in good time.

Gropings, orientations, crumbs, fragments, bits of the jigsaw, a few demented ravings that may help the reconstruction of the lost message. I am just beginning to regain my memory, just beginning to realize I am lost, just getting faint sounds of old familiar music – snatches of old tunes, moments of *déjà vu*, a reawakening of a long numbed agony – an unendurable realization of what a débâcle it was, what a shambles, what betrayal, horror, stupidity, ignorance, cowardice, craven lust, wretched greed. Faint recall of a raving nostalgia, for the Kingdom, the Power and the Glory, Paradise Lost. . . .

We tramps have so lost our wits we do not know what to steal, or even how to beg. We are the bereft. Derelicts.

Fishes, washed up and out in their death throes twitching rubbing themselves together for their own slime. Don't be a shy fish. This is no time for dignity or heroics. Our best hope is in cowardice and treachery. I would rather even be white than dead.

Mid-ocean. Shipwreck. Survivors are being picked up. The crew are saved but not the Captain-Governor-The Boss. The rescue ship moves away from the scene. Empty, still, desolate ocean. Slow track over surface. Suddenly, like a bird, I swoop down. There is the Captain. Is he dead? A sodden doll just afloat and no more. If he is not already dead, it seems he will certainly drown soon. Suddenly he is washed up at a fishing village. The fishermen don't know whether he is alive or dead, a captain or a doll or a queer fish. A doctor comes along, guts him open like a fish, or rips him open like a doll. There is a sodden, grey little man inside. Artificial respiration. He moves. He reddens with blood. Maybe he will make it.

How careful I must be! What a near thing! If only this really is the King coming back again. The Captain come to take over command. Now I can start up again. Putting things in order. Repairs, reconstructions, projects. Plans. Campaigns. Oh Yes.

There is another region of the soul called America.

It is impossible to express America. That last night was quite something a highly intelligent gathering so very white so very jewish i began to realize i was sat beside a bust in something like terracotta of perhaps a buddha. It was calm and still saying nothing doing nothing i further began to realize that there was a light coming from the top of its head a sixty watt electric bulb indeed i kid you not it was a lampstand.

What the fuck are you doing with a buddha as a lampstand?

O that's not a buddha that's some high goddess or other.

There presides over America a female effete laughing Buddha – fat beyond reason or imagination – creased with myriad folds and convolutions. The fat is on the turn. This she-Buddha is compounded of some cosmic muck and that is now fibrillating with monstrous pruritic desire. Millions of men fall on her to fuck away her unspeakable and insatiable obscene itch. They all get lost in the endless, greasy, fatty morass of her rancid recesses.

This writing is not exempt. It remains like all writing an absurd and revolting effort to make an impression on a world that will remain as unmoved as it is avid. If I could turn you on, if I could drive you out of your wretched mind, if I could tell you, I would let you know.

Who is not engaged in trying to impress, to leave a mark, to engrave his image on the others and the world – graven images held more dear than life itself? We wish to die leaving our imprints burned into the hearts of the others. What would life be if there were no one to remember us, to think of us when we are absent, to keep us alive when we are dead? And when we are dead, suddenly or gradually, our presence, scattered in ten or ten thousand hearts will fade and disappear. How many candles in how many hearts? Of such stuff is our hope and our despair.

How do you plug a void plugging a void? How to inject nothing into fuck all? How to come into a gone world? No piss, shit, smegma, come, mucoid, viscoid, soft or hard, or even tears of eyes, ears, arse, cunt, prick, nostrils, done to any T, of man or alligator, tortoise, or daughter, will plug up the Hole. It's gone past all that, that, all that last desperate clutch. Come into gone. I do assure you. The dreadful has already happened.

> Debris
> The old style
> All those endearing. . . .

I want you to taste and smell me, want to be palpable, to get under your skin, to be an itch in your brain and in your guts that you can't scratch out and that you can't allay, that will corrupt and destroy you and drive you mad. Who can write entirely with unadulterated compassion? All prose, all poetry, to the extent that it is not compassion, is failure.

Watch it. Care. Calm. Caution. Don't try it on too much, don't exploit it. Just keep your place, just don't ask for trouble. Remember your hands have blood on them, just don't be too cheeky, or too greedy. Don't puff yourself up too much. Remember your place in the hierarchy, don't try to come it, don't shout about, don't posture, don't give yourself airs, don't think you're going to get away with it, you've had a bit of the piss taken out of you, don't make excuses. Don't kick it around. Who are you trying to kid? A little humility, a fraction of love, a grain of trust, you've been told as much as you

need to know, you've had quite your fair share, don't try
the patience of the gods. Shut up and get on with it.
Remember. There's not much time left. The flood and the
fire are upon us.

> Yes, there are moments
> Sometimes
>   there is magic

> Winch with a smile
> Nothing so becomes a man

> That forlorn faiblesse
> That gentle nostalgia

> *Ich grolle nicht*

> Tenderness too is possible
> Ah tenderness

Wandering
Suddenly I come upon one of my many childhoods
Preserved in forgetfulness
For this moment when it was most required

He and she

A sad little tune
Its fingers so tentatively reach out towards our
    untouchable happiness,
Its very gentle smile so tactfully offers
Consolation we do not ask for.

SHE: My heart is full of ashes and lemon peel.
HE: Do not go too far away.
SHE: I shall only go into my self. You will always find me
    there.
HE: If I loved the whole world as I love you, I would die.

Forests and cataracts of intricate interstitial
  landscapes,
Cascades and waterfalls through and past
  elbows to promontories of fingers,
Star of nerves, arteries of champagne,
Her image tingles my fingertips,
Uncoils my recoiling flesh,
Touches a lost nerve of courage,
Entices an uncertain gesture of delight
To adventure into being.

The dance begins. Worms underneath fingertips, lips
beginning to pulse, heartache and throatcatch. All slightly out of step and out of key, each its own tempo and
rhythm. Slowly, connexions. Lip to lip, heart to heart,
finding self in other, dreadfully, tentatively, burningly . . .
notes finding themselves in chords, chords in sequence,
cacophony turning to polyphonous contrapuntal chorus,
a diapason of celebration.

Dancing waves of fluent highs and lows of lips and
nipples, fingers, spines, thighs, laughing, intertwining,
intermingling, fusing, and somewhere touched, an ultimate joy and gladness, lovely lightful life diffusing an ever
newer fiercer freshness. Yes this is possible, where from or
where to no more need to ask, him and her, you and me,
become us – more than a moment of us and a not too
despairing declension. What more is there to ask?

Tidal wave one million miles high moving at speed of
light. Impossible to go above or beneath, to run away, to
get round to left or right. The Government fires the land
with massive flame throwers, earth to desert, to absorb
the water. Fire against Water. Don't panic.

Tesselated marble at gate of Sixth Heaven may be
mistaken for water.

Garden. Cat at bird. Shoo off nasty cat, and catch bird. How elusive she is, and I am turning into a cat myself. Stop. Cat is a cat is a bird is a non-bird of ineffably frail space suddenly spreading in parabolic grace of authority. How foolish to worry, to try to save her, or grasp her. Perhaps the cat was trying to save her. Let be. Cat and bird. Begriff. The truth I am trying to grasp is the grasp that is trying to grasp it.

I have seen the Bird of Paradise, she has spread herself before me, and I shall never be the same again.

There is nothing to be afraid of. Nothing.

Exactly.

The Life I am trying to grasp is the me that is trying to grasp it.

There is really nothing more to say when we come back to that beginning of all beginnings that is nothing at all. Only when you begin to lose that Alpha and Omega do you want to start to talk and to write, and then there is no end to it, words, words, words. At best and most they are perhaps *in memoriam*, evocations, conjurations, incantations, emanations, shimmering, iridescent flares in the sky of darkness, a just still feasible tact, indiscretions, perhaps forgivable. . . .

City lights at night, from the air, receding, like these words, atoms each containing its own world and every other world. Each a fuse to set you off. . . .

If I could turn you on, if I could drive you out of your wretched mind, If I could tell you I would let you know.

MORE ABOUT PENGUINS
AND PELICANS

Penguinews, which appears every month, contains details of all the new books issued by Penguins as they are published. From time to time it is supplemented by *Penguins in Print*, which is our complete list of almost 5,000 titles.

A specimen copy of *Penguinews* will be sent to you free on request. Please write to Dept EP, Penguin Books Ltd, Harmondsworth, Middlesex, for your copy.

In the U.S.A.: For a complete list of books available from Penguins in the United States write to Dept CS, Penguin Books, 625 Madison Avenue, New York, New York 10022.

In Canada: For a complete list of books available from Penguins in Canada write to Penguin Books Canada Ltd, 41 Steelcase Road West, Markham, Ontario.

R. D. Laing

THE POLITICS OF THE FAMILY
AND OTHER ESSAYS

Standing, as *New Society* comments, 'rocklike above the ruck of the bounteous and bland psychological texts which pour from the presses', *The Politics of the Family*, in fellowship with the rest of R. D. Laing's works, adds a new dimension to our understanding of everyday situations.

In these essays the author crystallizes his thoughts on the family unit, schizophrenia in the family and on psychiatric intervention. He is not concerned with the necessity for action but, rather, with making the reader aware of his own innate assumptions, projections and introjections; and to help him to achieve an insight which, if it cannot be entirely truthful, is, at least, not entirely confused.

'Dr Laing's brilliant unravelling of the knots perhaps makes these particular writings the most generally significant in England in the last decade' – *The Times Educational Supplement*

R. D. Laing

THE DIVIDED SELF

The Divided Self is a unique study of the human situation.

Dr Laing's first purpose is to make madness and the process of going mad comprehensible. In this, with case studies of schizophrenic patients, he succeeds brilliantly, but he does more; through a vision of sanity and madness as 'degrees of conjunction and disjunction between two persons where the one is sane by common consent' he offers a rich existential analysis of personal alienation.

The outsider, estranged from himself and society, cannot experience either himself or others as 'real'. He invents a false self and with it he confronts both the outside world and his own despair. The disintegration of his real self keeps pace with the growing unreality of his false self until, in the extremes of schizophrenic breakdown, the whole personality disintegrates.

'Dr Laing is saying something very important indeed ... This is a truly humanist approach' – Philip Toynbee in the *Observer*

'It is a study that makes all other works I have read on schizophrenia seem fragmentary ... The author brings, through his vision and perception, that particular touch of genius which causes one to say "Yes, I have always known that, why have I never thought of it before?"'– *Journal of Analytical Psychology*

Also published

SELF AND OTHERS

SANITY, MADNESS AND THE FAMILY
(R. D. Laing and A. Esterson)